The Silent Dialogue

The Silent Dialogue

Zen Letters
to a Trappist Abbot

David G. Hackett

CONTINUUM • NEW YORK

1996

The Continuum Publishing Company
370 Lexington Avenue
New York, NY 10017

Printed in the United States of America

Library of Congress Cataloging-in-Publication Data

Hackett, David G.
   The silent dialogue : Zen letters to a Trappist abbot / David. G.
Hackett.
      p.   cm.
   ISBN 0-8264-0780-3 (hardcover : alk. paper)
   1. Zen Buddhism—Relations—Catholic Church. 2. Catholic
Church—Relations—Zen Buddhism. 3. Spiritual life—Zen
Buddhism. 4. Spiritual life—Catholic Church. I. Title.
BQ9269.4.C35H33 1996
261.2'43927—dc20   96-27333
                                                          CIP

To Thomas Keating

You are so young, so before all beginning,
and I want to beg you, as much as I can,
to be patient toward all that
is unsolved in your heart
and try to love the
questions themselves
like locked rooms and
like books that are written
in a very foreign tongue.
Do not seek the answers,
which cannot be given you
because you would not
be able to live them.
And the point is,
to live everything.
Live the questions now.
Perhaps you will then gradually,
without noticing it, live along
some distant day into the answer

— Rainer Maria Rilke

Contents

Acknowledgments

In the fall of 1995, I received a letter from a friend who had become interested in Zen. She asked if I could recommend a book for her to read. Looking over the shelves of my study, I ran across the manuscript that has become this book. In 1976, as a way of bringing to a close a chapter in my life, I had assembled my correspondence with Father Thomas Keating and the monks at St. Joseph's, the Trappist monastery in Spencer, Massachusetts, into a typed manuscript, and put it on my shelf. I had not looked at it again in twenty years. I took it home that night to read and then, thinking it might be helpful, sent it to my friend. Soon after she responded and encouraged me to publish it. When the book was accepted for publication, I began to realize that now I had to confront my twenty-five-year-old self from the perspective of twenty years.

This has been a rewarding process, through which I have reopened an important period in my life and renewed some wonderful friendships. For their encouragement and counsel in editing the original manuscript, I thank Sara Wuthnow, Chris Coates, and Robin Sweat. Wendy Young, my wife, was particularly helpful in encouraging me not to obscure my personal struggles in intellectualizing. I also want to thank Frank Oveis, my editor at Continuum, for bringing this book to publication. Though the subtitle's "Zen Letters" did not sit well with me, I understood his effort to communicate the gist of the book's content in a short, direct phrase. Finally, I am delighted that the process of publication has put me back in touch with a wonderful community of Trappist monks, both at Spencer and at Snowmass. I especially want to thank Raphael, Basil, William, Edward John, Kevin, Simon, and Jim for reading the manuscript and offering their corrections and encouragement. I dedicate this book to Father Thomas, who continues to touch my life with love and wisdom.

Prologue

During the late sixties and early seventies, a growing number of young people began turning up at St. Joseph's Trappist[1] Monastery in Spencer, Massachusetts, looking for a spirituality that they could experience. This was a time when a great many people were heading East or turning East, a process that many still do, to find in other traditions what they felt was missing in their own. Some of these people had experienced the radical politics, psychedelic drugs, communal living, and Eastern religions of the sixties counterculture, and now, Catholic and non-Catholic alike, they were "checking out" Catholic monasticism to see what spiritual goods might be found there. During this same time period, Abbot Thomas Keating and the monks at Spencer were experimenting with Eastern religious practices as part of their effort to update and renew the life of their Cistercian Order of the Strict Observance subsequent to the reforms of Vatican II. I was one of these young seekers who came out of the sixties counterculture to encounter the Spencer community in the midst of its opening to the East.

I first visited Spencer in the fall of 1971, during my sophomore year at Amherst College. A reading course I had been taking on alternative spiritual communities led me to the writings of the Trappist monk, Thomas Merton. This initial encounter, however, was preceded by several years of participation in the counterculture. I was raised in an academic, humanist environment. My father was a professor at the University of Michigan, and he and my mother encouraged me to seek my own answers. At Amherst I had participated in the Vietnam war protests and experimented with various ways to alter consciousness. The latter experiences, in particular, opened my awareness to the existence of a transcendent, spiritual world beyond my ordinary reality.

---

1. Trappists are the monks of the Cistercian Order of the Strict Observance. The former name derives from an eighteenth-century reform instituted at La Trappe in France.

During the summer and fall of 1970, I left school to join an alternative community called Cumbres (Spanish for "mountain peak") in southern New Hampshire as part of my effort to explore this new spiritual world through psychological and religious practices. Visitors to Cumbres included the Harvard psychologist-turned-guru Ram Dass, the Carmelite contemplative Friar William McNamara, proponents of the new group therapies, and other psychological and spiritual leaders of the day. On my return to college, I was even more intent on discovering for myself a way of living that would incorporate spiritual practice. One late November night, while reading one of Merton's books, I found a map of the Trappist monasteries in the United States and noticed that Spencer was just down the road from Amherst. And right then, that very night, I decided to set out for the monastery and become a monk.

It was premature winter in the Berkshire foothills—windy, wet, and freezing cold on that November night I first ascended the steep road to the monastery. The further I climbed into the wooded hills, the more a deepening silence enclosed me and drove my imagination to extremes. My image of a monk was one of fiery eyes and redwood stature, and I believed I saw such ethereal giants walking in deep thought through every wooded glen I passed. I took the path leading to the guesthouse and apprehensively approached the old wooden door. After ringing once I waited, then rang once more. Presently I heard a shuffling behind the door and then, as in some fairy tale, a monk appeared. He wore a white robe and black hood, smiled, and motioned me inside.

I had surprisingly little explaining to do, for it seemed that I was expected. Rather than interrogate me, he immediately began to attend to my needs. Had I eaten? Slept? And, looking down at my sandals, was I cold? I responded negatively to the latter two and he led me to a nearby Victorian-style sitting room. I could sleep there, the monk said, and he would awaken me for the Lauds office (communal morning prayer) at six-thirty. I wasn't asked anything else. It seemed not the first time that a young man had arrived in such a manner. My motives, though unspoken, seemed understood. Bidding me goodnight, the monk shuffled off down the corridor, leaving me with a warm couch in a comfortable room. The fact that I was in a monastery when, just four hours before, I had been at college was certainly peculiar, but so much had been out of the ordinary in my life of the past few years that being in a monastery seemed more like the next step in a peculiar series of illogical events than a single isolated incident.

Sleep came quickly and it seemed as if many hours passed before the monk who had met me at the door, Brother Paschal, came to wake me for the Lauds office and morning Mass. Rather than take me outside to the visitors' gallery, Paschal said he would lead me through the monastery to the back of the church where I could see everything. I suppose I should have been excited about going through the inside of the monastery, but I was terrified. Passing beyond those "no admittance" signs, I imagined, would be like going down *Alice in Wonderland's* rabbit hole, down to a Never-Never Land of incense, fasting, and holy chanting. I was trembling, but Paschal had turned to lead and I had no choice but to follow.

Walking a labyrinth of corridors and doors with a crucifix at every turn, we approached the central cloister. Silently we passed through a kitchen, hallway, chapel, library, and on through yet another corridor. The monks we passed were of all shapes and ages and all dressed in the black hood and white robe of Brother Paschal. As we rounded the last turn and entered the long, windowed cloister that led to the church, I became certain that I was down the rabbit's hole. In the corridor to my left was an elderly monk walking slowly to the rhythm of rosary beads held behind his back; in the cloister garden was another one lost in prayer looking up at a tree. As we approached the church there were several who sat on benches reading books or simply tucked into their hoods looking quietly out into the garden. All of this was so different from my own life that I felt like screaming and running for the nearest door, but who knew where that would lead? I followed Paschal and we entered the church.

I did whatever Paschal did. When he crossed himself after entering, so did I; when he bowed before the altar, so did I. He showed me where to sit and I stood until I saw him sit. Ten yards in front of me were two rows of monks facing each other. My eyes darted from the altar to the organ to the individual monks. They were bearded and clean-shaven, young and old, fat and thin, all types, a cross-section of New England men. But where they differed in outer appearance they all seemed joined in purpose. There was an unearthly peace on their faces and in the church.

The office began with a prayer and continued with a song. The ritual was choreographed to include moments of recitation while sitting, followed by standing and singing, then sitting and listening to another reading, and finally standing again in silent prayer. It did not take long for me to become entranced by this dance of words, song, and silence. Sitting back, I allowed myself to relax and soon was lulled to sleep.

I awoke with a start when my name was spoken. Up there in the choir, Brother Paschal had asked the others to pray for David Hackett. And they answered, "Lord hear our prayer." No longer a spectator, I was part of the Mass. These men recognized me and perhaps even cared for me. Inwardly

I wept. My fatigue and mental confusion culminated in this moment of joy and relief. I felt their care.

After Mass Brother Paschal led me back down the corridors to the guesthouse and my sitting room. He told me that breakfast would be ready in a few moments and that I should wait there. It was now nearly eight o'clock and, for the first time, my rational mind began to dominate and remind me of my daily schedule of classes back at college. This train of thought was further reinforced by my conversation with the monk who came to visit me right after breakfast. He started asking all those questions of motivation which Brother Paschal had so kindly avoided. Most embarrassing was this monk's discovery that I was neither a Catholic nor had I ever been baptized into any Christian denomination. This was certainly true, but I also thought it was peripheral to my reasons for being there. I tried to explain to him how I had come the previous evening, and I thought he would surely understand why I had come as I did. But rather than nod in understanding, he seemed to withdraw and began to treat me as more sick than seeking. Perhaps he was right, but his actions immediately cooled any religious impulse I had afire within me and instead brought to the fore those rational arguments for getting back to school.

I left that morning, though the unearthly peace and beauty of the monastery stayed with me and, several weeks later, I returned. This time I was met by the abbot, Father Thomas, a tall, thin man in his fifties, whose serene and reassuring manner supported and affirmed my nascent spiritual seeking. He talked of his nephews and their college adjustments. I spoke of my wanderings and desire for a spiritual home. Casually we walked outside and around the grounds, the abbot's simple humanity doing much to dispel my fantastic illusions about the monastic world. To Thomas the fact that I was not a Christian mattered less than his recognition that I was indeed on a spiritual journey. Offering his support and guidance, Father Thomas asked nothing in return.

My response to Thomas's support and care was to ask to know more about the Catholic faith. For several weeks I returned to the monastery to study the catechism with him. During these meetings the abbot emanated a serenity that made any moment with him memorable; before long, however, studying the church's teachings became an arduous task. The catechism told me that faith meant to believe in something that I had never seen nor experienced. I could not do that. And so, though I continued to find in my meetings with Thomas the peace I thought I was seeking, I stopped coming to the abbey.

Gradually now my interest turned to Zen meditation. I first heard of Zen when it came into vogue in the late sixties. Then, while a college freshman, I read Philip Kapleau's *The Three Pillars of Zen*[2] and tried, unsuccessfully, to follow the author's meditation instructions. My attraction to a Japanese form of meditation probably had something to do with the fact that my father was raised in Japan, the son of Protestant missionaries. After leaving Japan, he had become a professor of Japanese history and left behind the formal religious training of his earlier years. During my childhood our family took three separate year-long trips to Japan, the last encompassing my junior year in high school. Despite this family background and initial exposure to Zen writings, I lost interest in Zen after my freshman year. After I ended my discussions with Father Thomas, however, the interest returned. In the summer before I began a year of graduate study in education at Harvard, I embarked on a two-week retreat at the Mt. Baldy Zen Center in southern California. This newfound interest in Zen meditation then led me back to Spencer, where I hoped to find some explanation about where my meditation was leading.

The practice of Zen meditation helped me to enter into the spiritual experiences I had first touched on in the counterculture and had encountered again at the Spencer monastery. My understanding of Zen, however, did not provide me with a clear explanation for where my journey was taking me. Through meditation I imagined that I would be led to an ever deeper peace, but just how this would happen remained a mystery. I realized that I needed advice from someone who was farther along this road than I, someone who would be receptive to my questions but would not impose his own point of view. I had received such advice once before from Father Thomas. So with nothing to lose, I wrote to him explaining my current situation and asked if I could come again to visit.

Father Thomas not only welcomed my visit but also informed me that in the time since our last conversation he had become interested in the practice of Zen meditation to deepen Christian faith. In fact, Sasaki Roshi, the Japanese Zen master of the Mt. Baldy Zen Center, had already given two retreats to the monks at Spencer. Now when I visited there I joined in not only with the monks in the Divine offices in the church but also with the little band of brothers doing Zen meditation together in the chapter (community meeting) room during the early morning hours.

---

2. Philip Kapleau, *The Three Pillars of Zen* (New York: Harper and Row, 1969).

Throughout that year of graduate school I continued to visit Father Thomas and meditate with the monks. I was permitted to stay at the little cottage within the monastery's grounds and increasingly join in the work and prayer rhythm of their contemplative life. Following my year at Harvard, I asked to participate in the monastery's new "residency" program. This program allowed lay people to participate in the life of the monastery for three months to a year. I would be the second participant in this program and was invited to stay for three months. As the "strangeness" of monasticism became familiar and the spiritual world the monks inhabited felt more and more like home, I became interested once again in converting to the Catholic faith that gave meaning to their life.

My struggle with conversion centered on my resistance to surrendering myself to God. All during the spring of 1974 and on through my first month in the monastery, I found it difficult to relax my mind and trust in God. I did not see how I could believe in God without first experiencing God. And I did not see how I could truly understand Christianity without first spending many years in contemplative practice. Father Thomas responded that it was true that in one lifetime I would never exhaust the riches of the wisdom of God embodied in Christ. Still, I had to begin somewhere. Christ presents himself to us not only as the End, Thomas said, but also as the Way ("I am the Way, the Truth, and the Life"). As he put it in a letter:

> To believe in the ultimate reality embodied in Jesus without understanding it is exactly what faith means. Faith is a surrender. It is a surrender not only of our mind, which adheres to Christ's words as the revelation of God without fully understanding them or even without understanding them at all. It is also the surrender of our life, to be guided and moved inwardly and outwardly by Christ through his Spirit which he gives to those who believe. This kind of faith is a gift. We can only ask for it with humble hope.

Through Thomas's guidance I came to see that faith would come to me, but not through the ordinary means of the senses, imagination or feelings. It was not for me to seek to procure faith, rather it would be granted to me. Still, I resisted this surrender.

While this struggle went on, I continued to be immersed in the silence of monastic daily life and observing the monks at work. Each was a man who appeared to have committed his life to resolving the questions that I had only begun to raise. The spiritual lives led by these monks were gradually becoming the most powerful influences upon my Catholic leaning. The more secure I felt with them, the more acceptable I found their faith.

My interest in Zen developed because it was an effective method for coming to quiet; my interest in Christianity had grown because of my contact
with Cistercian monks. However, I did not then consider myself either a
Buddhist or a Christian. I tended to regard Buddhism and Christianity as
parallel means to a common end. To become a Christian I would have to
accept that Jesus was and is the Son of God. I would also have to agree that
Christianity and Buddhism are not coequal because God's designs for the
world were overtly revealed in Christ and not in Buddha. I found these
claims intolerable.

And then one day in late June, Father Raphael, an older monk, spoke
with me about Catholic dogma. He said that dogma ultimately means *mystery*. The mystery, Raphael said, is the revelation hidden in God which he
manifests to us, and through whose manifestation he brings about our sal-
vation and sanctification: the fulfillment of his design. This mystery is
beyond our intellectual grasp, he continued, and must be revealed to be
known by us and then received by faith. My understanding of what Father
Raphael said helped me to reach a far less hostile view of Catholic teachings than I had heretofore thought possible. As I understood him, the mystery of dogma is initially revealed to us through the church's teachings and
the first act of faith is an intellectual assent to these teachings. As we grow
in faith, however, we transform our intellectual understanding of dogma
into a spiritual experience that can probe infinitely deeper into dogma's
mystery. Catholic teachings were like the gateway to an ever deepening
mystery impossible to express in words. So rather than quibble with words,
I thought, it was better that I try to grasp the mystery behind the teachings
by "waiting" for God, as I had been all along, in my Zen meditation.

It was also at this time that a strange consoling calm descended upon
me. Every day of that first week in July I thought of baptism. After one
month at the monastery I was ready to conclude that I could not live a spiritual life by relying solely upon my own resources, yet neither could I
expect God to do all the work. Yielding to the abbot, to monastic regula-
tions, and ultimately to God, I recognized my submission to higher
authorities. Faith seemed to grow through bankruptcy. First a total expen-
diture of my own resources; and then, in my weakness, surrender to whatever God wanted me to do.

On the first Sunday of July, I went to speak with the abbot about baptism. Father Thomas said that in order for me to be baptized I must surrender my will to God. He had said this to me many times before, but I had
never really understood what he meant. This time though, I was ready to
hear him. Rather than nod my head in agreement, I felt a sudden rush of

emotion run through me. It was as if my whole being was nodding in agreement. Soon, however, other voices within me began to marshal emotional support for an all-out attack against baptism.

When I had first considered baptism, several years before, these same voices had made short work of my desire for conversion. Now, though the intellectual doubts had subsided, there was still an emotional struggle. That evening and most of the next day I felt weighed down by a feeling of enslavement to God. Every moment seemed tinged with a rotten, gloomy feeling of defeat. My ego felt tricked and hated it.

While this struggle went on, other events conspired to bring about conversion. At the Vespers office on Monday, the reading was about the happy yet arduous conversion of a nineteenth-century Frenchman. Lines like "absurd choice" and "ludicrous yet courageous decision" hit home. At dinner there was a note at my place with the following line from Merton: "Prayer and love become possible in the hour when it is impossible to pray and your heart has turned to stone."

Still, parts of me wanted no part of Christianity. I became mocking and bitter and wanted to do something outrageous like drop my choir book and stomp out during Mass. The selfish feeling of injustice homed in on me. I would not enslave myself to this mythical God!

The next morning I poured out my frustrations in a talk with Father Thomas. He responded by telling me to take it easy and that I should not attack the problem so urgently that I drain my mental and emotional resources. He went on to ask, "What precisely is it that you are so afraid of losing? Could it be that you have a strong attachment to your own proud self-image and that is the thing you are so afraid of losing if you submit yourself completely to God? Is losing that really a loss? Rather than losing anything really worthwhile, you might be gaining a greater freedom and independence than you have now." These words, spoken firmly, ripped right through me. In an instant they seemed to burst my blister of egotism and wash the resistance out of the sore. It was as if all my searching culminated in that one moment. All the energy now seemed to drain out of my body, leaving me weak.

I made it back to my room, sat down in my chair, and stared blankly out the window. Neither contentment nor relief came to me, just a calm, invisible presence that made me feel that I was not there, as if I had disappeared. I felt naked, shattered, stripped of all my defenses, unable to do anything about it, and not wanting to do anything anyway. What two days before had seemed like cruel abuse now felt honey sweet. I felt detached from the "me" that I had always thought I was. Instead I felt sheltered amidst a beauty that I had never before experienced. A line from that day's Lauds office came to me: "For we know that if the earthly tent we live in is destroyed, we have a building from God" (2 Cor 5:1).

One month later I was formally baptized, though psychologically my baptism took place during those few days in early July. The climax had been reached and passed. Still the ceremony symbolized formal recognition of my experience. Papers were signed, vows made, and every monk at the monastery was witness to those vows. Intellectually I followed the six separate rites of exorcism that preceded the church ceremony and occurred on separate days. I listened closely as Father Thomas explained the profound mysteries that were then inscribed in my soul. Yet the depth and import of these mysteries placed them far beyond my experience, so that I could only gratefully accept them and hope someday to understand them.

Perhaps the greatest solace though was the feeling that I had begun. I had finally entered into a definite path and spiritual practice. All of my previous wanderings were but preparations for my baptism, and baptism was just the entry gate to an ever deepening mystery.

Δ

And so it was in August of 1974, in the sanctuary of the Spencer monastery, that I reached what seemed to be the end of my journey by finding my way into the Catholic Church. My conversion was the culmination of a series of inquiries that had Zen meditation as their most constant thread. I became a Catholic through Zen meditation and an understanding of the Catholic faith afforded me by the patient guidance of Father Thomas. Rather than my quest ending in conversion, however, baptism opened a new series of questions and marked the beginning of a new inquiry.

As my exposure to Zen and the church developed, I had begun reading the few books available on Zen and Catholicism. What I learned was that the first of these were written in the mid-sixties and compared the insights of the great mystics of Christianity and Buddhism. The English Benedictine abbot Aelred Graham's *Zen Catholicism* (1963) and Thomas Merton's *Mystics and Zen Masters* (1967) raised the possibility of applying the insights of Zen to Catholicism. After Vatican II's exhortation to engage in dialogue with non-Christian religions (1965), both of these men wrote books that began the work of comparing Christianity and Buddhism through dialogue with Buddhist leaders. Thomas Merton's *Zen and the Birds of Appetite* (1968) included a long discussion between Merton and D. T.

Suzuki, the early Japanese apostle of Zen to the United States. Aelred Graham's *Conversations: Christian and Buddhist* (1968) recounted thirteen discussions he had with representatives of Buddhism in Japan.

As dialogue came to the forefront in the late sixties, the Zen–Catholic focus moved to a trio of Jesuits on the faculty of Sophia University in Tokyo. In 1970, William Johnston wrote *The Still Point*, which grew out of his participation in the yearly Buddhist–Christian dialogues begun in Kyoto in 1968. This was followed by *Christian Zen* (1971) and a book by Johnston's colleague, H. M. Enomiya Lassalle, *Zen Meditation for Christians* (1974). An earlier work, *Zen: Way to Enlightenment*, had been published by Lassalle in 1968. Each of these offered practical instruction and theological reassurance for the Christian interested in practicing Zen meditation. A third Jesuit at Sophia, Heinrich Dumoulin, drew on his lifelong study of Zen Buddhism, his experience as an adviser to Vatican II's Committee on Non-Christian Religions, and his primary involvement in the Buddhist–Christian dialogue to produce the landmark *Christianity Meets Buddhism* (1974), which marked the progress and possibilities of Christian–Buddhist interaction in Japan to that date.[3]

In the early 1970s the monks of St. Joseph's Abbey had begun to look into Zen, as well as Yoga and Transcendental Meditation, as part of their response to the greater freedom and pluralism encouraged by Vatican II. Through the guidance of Father Thomas, they had been exposed to Zen meditation in the retreats led by Sasaki Roshi and several monks had eagerly read through the small but growing library of books on Christianity and the East. During my three months in the monastery, I meditated with these monks and consulted with Father Thomas on the efficacy of Zen meditation for Christians. Judging from what we read, experienced, and heard, we were fairly certain that Zen meditation could be beneficial to many Christians who desired a contemplative practice.

The use of a Buddhist technique to deepen Christian faith, however, was a new step and one that raised numerous questions that we alone

---

3.   Aelred Graham, *Zen Catholicism: A Suggestion* (New York: Harcourt, Brace, and World, 1963); Thomas Merton, *Mystics and Zen Masters* (New York: Farrar, Strauss, and Giroux, 1967); Thomas Merton, *Zen and the Birds of Appetite* (New York: New Directions, 1968); Aelred Graham, *Conversations: Christian and Buddhist* (New York: Harcourt, Brace, and World, 1968); William Johnston, *The Still Point: Reflections on Zen and Christian Mysticism* (New York: Fordham University Press, 1970) and *Christian Zen* (New York: Harper and Row, 1971); H. M. Enomiya Lassalle, *Zen Meditation for Christians* (LaSalle, Ill.: Open Court, 1974) and *Zen: Way to Enlightenment* (New York: Taplinger, 1968); Heinrich Dumoulin, *Christianity Meets Buddhism* (LaSalle, Ill.: Open Court, 1974).

could not answer. The previous spring I had decided to go to Japan after my stay at the abbey to pursue these questions further. I wanted to get a better understanding of Zen, how it related to Buddhism, and how it could best be employed to deepen Christian faith. Two weeks after my conversion in the monastery, I left for Japan and eventually Southeast Asia. There I hoped to talk with Zen masters sympathetic to Catholicism and Catholic priests who were delving into Zen. I also wanted to visit Zen temples which welcomed westerners and Catholic institutions open to Buddhist influences. I planned as well to keep an eye out for signs of new forms of Catholic religious life that could be built around Zen meditation.

My earlier trips with my family helped me to feel familiar with Japan. During the first year of my journey, my parents would be spending their regular sabbatical year in Kyoto, the cultural capital of Japan. I was going to live an hour away in the large, industrial city of Nagoya, where I had a job as a high school teacher at an international school. I planned to spend my weekends and vacations consulting whomever I could and keeping in touch with the Trappists back in Massachusetts.

The material for this book is primarily drawn from the series of letters that I sent to Father Thomas and the monks of St. Joseph's Abbey during my two-year stay in Japan and the subsequent summer's travel through Southeast Asia. Each chapter includes one or more of these letters, which were written in journal form, with several dated entries, and sent to Spencer at odd intervals. I have also included excerpts from letters sent by Father Thomas and some of the monks in response. These chapters reflect my changing experience with Zen meditation and Christianity. It is the voice of a young man on a spiritual journey and still troubled by issues of being in the world. I wanted to feel at peace with my Catholic practice of Zen meditation and I hoped to find a community life that would encourage Zen practice within the Catholic faith. Where these interests led me in those two years is the concern of this book.

Part I

Japan

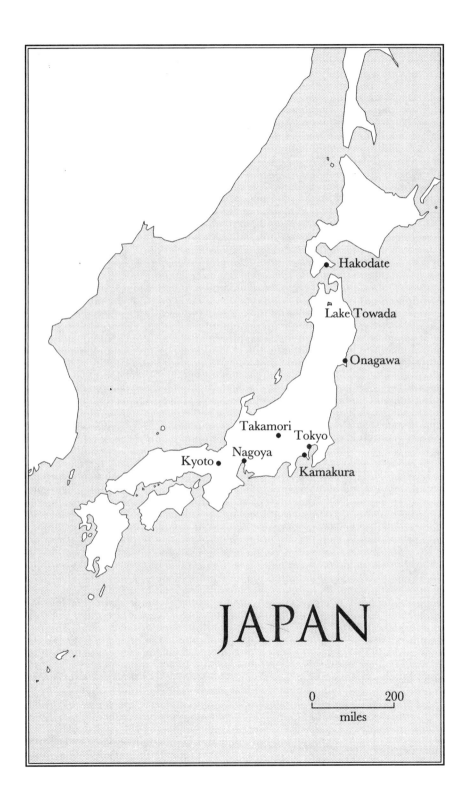

Hakodate

Lake Towada

Onagawa

Takamori Tokyo

Nagoya

Kyoto

Kamakura

JAPAN

0   200

miles

Tie Your Camels First

September 10, 1974, Nagoya, Japan[1]

I have had it on my mind to write ever since I left the monastery three weeks ago, but first I thought that I would allow my vision to clear. Yet my perception remains blurred.

What I mean to say is that I have a great deal of orientation to undergo on a number of levels. My life in Nagoya is now like a jigsaw puzzle for which I possess only a few parts. The rest must be imagined. For instance, I have no sure grasp of the surrounding geography. My connecting flight from Tokyo has plunked me down in Nagoya, which is somewhere in central Japan, closer to Kyoto than Tokyo, but that is all I really know. Teaching at the Nagoya International School is a new experience, and how to motivate my students remains mysterious. The house that I live in is neither well organized nor fully furnished. I live on the periphery of a society which I cannot yet fathom. These are not serious problems, yet they are the immediate issues with which I must deal. There is a Sufi saying that advises: "When you go to climb the pyramid, tie your camels first." Before I can begin to pursue religious questions, I need to function normally. So there is much to figure out. Still, I suspect that in a month or so I will feel at home.

From the little information I have been able to gather, the Catholic situation in Nagoya is a small affair. The Sunday Mass in English is held in a small room on the second floor of the English Academy downtown. The

---

1. Unless otherwise indicated, each of these letters, usually encompassing several dated entries, were addressed to Father Thomas and the monks of St. Joseph's Abbey.

Academy is run by the Maryknoll Fathers (an American congregation of priests dedicated to foreign missions). Since I live more than fifteen miles outside of town, I cannot attend daily Mass. Perhaps I can find a Japanese church closer to my home. There are about fifteen foreign priests in Nagoya and perhaps as many as four times that number of Japanese priests spread throughout this broad city. I live on the city's outskirts, at the base of some foothills that signal the beginning of the Japan Alps—not all that scenic, but nice.

My spiritual situation is as murky as everything else, but like everything else it is more a problem of orientation than one of crisis. I miss going to daily Mass, my sitting is irregular, and there is a dearth of religious books in English. I do read the Gospels daily and occasionally say the rosary.

Scattered conversations about Zen and Christianity have repeatedly elicited the name of Father Lassalle as *the* authority on the subject. I hope to make it to his Zen–Catholic retreat house outside of Tokyo before Thanksgiving.

Another point that has come up in conversations is the lack of religious fervor among the Japanese. In fact, Tami, a Japanese convert who lives nearby, says that the man on the street professes no religion at all. The modern Japanese may well believe that the United States is the more religious country. The grass is always greener.

A Letter from Father Thomas

September 26, Spencer

Thanks for your letter of September 10. I can see you are struggling with the adjustment on many levels, but I'm glad to see that your customary optimism is still in the ascendancy. Evidently it is going to take a while to get to meet the key people with whom you are trying to get in contact. At least you can go on praying. I was glad to hear that you have continued to read the Gospels daily. I hope you can get back to regular sitting soon. If the full amount of time that you like is not possible, you can at least do a part of it; or try to offer yourself to God through some other method of prayer like the rosary, focusing your attention on the mystery of Christ beyond the mysteries.

Δ

September 24, Nagoya

Last weekend I went to Kyoto, seventy miles west of here, to see my parents. While there I attended Mass at a large midtown church. The service was in Japanese, so my poor language skills found me reciting the "Our Father" when it should have been the Creed. The frustration of my fumbling was more than overcome, however, by the beautiful female voices in the choir. Leaving the church I stopped to talk with a Maryknoll priest who stood outside to chat with foreigners new to Kyoto. We talked awhile about his missionary work, and then I told him of my interest in Zen. He said that he had recently met a German girl in Kyoto named Claudia who is a recent convert to Catholicism and also interested in Zen. The priest gave me her phone number, I called, and in three hours I was at her house.

Claudia is a big, cheerful German woman. Her spiritual search began with Transcendental Meditation. Then she was drawn to the Mass and began saying "Christe Eleison" (Christ Is Risen) as a prayer; she still considers the latter to be central to her prayer life. Throughout her search, however, she felt drawn to the East. After conversion, Claudia left her graduate work in Asian studies to come to Japan. Here she has become fascinated by *sumie* (black ink drawing), *ikebana* (flower arranging), and the tea ceremony. These interests, coupled with her new faith, have catapulted her into the silence and ceremony of Zen.

Interest in Zen took Claudia first to Father Lassalle's retreat house where, she tells me, Lassalle plays the role of a Zen master. There she met a German priest. He was sent to Lassalle by his bishop in Germany in order to bring Zen meditation back to his diocese. The fellow took one look at Claudia, a nice German woman interested in Zen, and decided that she was just the person he needed to help him teach this form of meditation back in Germany. Although he focuses his Zen training on Japanese converts, holding only one *sesshin* (a week of intensive meditation) each year in English, Father Lassalle is interested in mounting a beachhead for Christian Zen meditation in his native Germany.

After tea, served by Claudia in the proper Japanese manner, I got up to leave. In parting she offered to arrange through a friend of hers a visit for us with a *roshi* (Zen master) of whom we could ask our questions about combining *zazen* (the practice of Zen meditation) with the Catholic faith.

Δ

October 5, Nagoya

Got in my car and headed blindly north toward the Japan Alps. Slowly I began to pull away from the overpopulation and pollution that makes the southern rim of Japan's main island resemble one long Los Angeles. Turning on to the smaller roads that trailed off into the foothills of the coming mountains, the scenery took a more traditional turn. More dark cotton pants on the women in the fields, fewer machines, a quiet return to the old Japan. Mountainous foothills with long silent stretches of hillside loomed up at sharp angles austerely denying habitation. People and houses became fewer and the scenery that is the inspiration of so many early Japanese paintings came into view. Out there in the remote mystery of Japan's fabled back-country, the stranger with only his eyes to guide him can easily be convinced that Shinto has the greatest religious influence on the Japanese people.

The indigenous religion of Japan, Shinto, is a polytheistic nature worship. Anything which evokes a feeling of awe is revered as being particularly imbued with divine or mysterious power; the forces of nature, trees, mountains, ancestors, heroes, and others are all objects of worship. These are given the name *kami*. The Japanese approach kami in an aura of intimacy. They feel love and gratitude and the desire to console and placate, or so I have read.[2] The worshipper usually faces the object of devotion itself, perhaps a tree, stone, or even a sunrise, and simply stands quietly and bows to its presence—maybe lights a stick of incense or a candle. In time, a shrine might be erected at the spot or, if the object of worship is a distant mountain, a covering might be prepared under which the worshiper can stand. Shrines are usually of quite simple construction with few decorative effects, often just a thatched roof with pillar supports. Within there might be a symbolic representation of the deity imbued in the object of worship. The deity is frequently symbolized by a stone or a mirror. Invariably the shrine is marked off by a straw rope from which are attached small strips of paper that are said to fend off evil influences. Often nestled in a grove of trees, a shrine compound might be entered through a *torii*, a distinctive arched gateway that separates the sacred from the secular.

---

2. Several of the ideas presented here and in the following paragraphs are derived from a reading of *Religions in Japan*, edited by William K. Bunce, 98-102; this report was prepared by the Religions and Cultural Resources Division, Civil Information and Education Section, General Headquarters of the Supreme Commander for the Allied Powers in 1948 and published in 1955 by the Charles E. Tuttle Company in Tokyo.

Though Shinto has no official scripture, founder, or organized teaching, it remains today an important religious influence in Japan. Books I've read tell me that Shinto is a way of life inextricably woven into the texture of Japanese thought and conduct.

As I drove silently onward through the mountain villages and broad expanses of the Japan Alps, I was increasingly accompanied by a silent traveling partner, the ubiquitous Shinto shrine. It seemed that each turn in the road was marked off as holy ground. If torii did not announce larger shrines, little hollowed rocks, with a candle or two inside, quietly made note of a tree, a view, or waterfall of surpassing beauty.

As the indigenous religion, Shinto has at times become more an expression of "things Japanese" than an attempt to be a religion in the manner of Christianity or Buddhism. In Shinto's early development, the leader of the Yamato clan, the first group to consolidate the Japanese people, came to be revered as the chief priest of Shinto. The deification of the Yamato clan's leader led ultimately to esteem for the Japanese emperor as the leader of the Japanese people and, more zealously, the world. In the ideological build-up to World War II, the government required that all followers of religions other than Shinto show obeisance to their local Shinto shrine as a nonreligious expression of nationalism. Following the war, the awe and reverence for nature which is pure Shinto remains part of the Japanese character.

October 6, Nagoya

I have been reading an interesting little book by Uchiyama Roshi, the retired abbot of Antai-ji Zen Temple in Kyoto. The book is called *Approach to Zen*. This Zen master has dealt with foreigners at his temple for quite a few years. In his book Uchiyama Roshi tries first to dispel notions of the exotic in Zen monastic life. Books about Zen, he says, too frequently present either in pictures or in words a misty mountain scene which, though indeed is often the background in Zen's home city of Kyoto, offers only one aspect of Zen life. For when the fog and mist are cleared away by the light of reason, the roshi states, seekers of mist will all too frequently find themselves with a lot of oriental trivia and nonsense. Time and again Uchiyama Roshi drives home the point that mysticism should not be based on anti-intellectualism. Rather it should follow reason until it becomes obvious that the true depth of life comes at a point beyond the reach of the intellect.

Most interesting to me is one of the ideas offered near the end of the book. In drawing an important distinction between Buddhist and Christian explanations of belief, Uchiyama Roshi says that:

> In religion when an agent of God (medium) speaks suggestively about an invisible realm (a metaphysical realm) and says that there is such and such a God or that man has a soul, people assume that it is true and act accordingly. This is called "believing". But the basic Buddhist definition of "belief" is completely different . . . in Buddhism belief is not to hear somebody say that man has an individual Soul or that God does exist outside the life of the self and to think that this is so. . . Belief is clarity and purity . . . the very act of doing zazen is to believe."[3]

Belief, I gather, is affirmation through experience rather than affirmation through faith.

My hunch is that a Christian explanation of belief includes the Buddhist definition given by Uchiyama Roshi but goes further. When Christians do zazen, they are believing in the Buddhist sense; however, their spiritual growth is not dependent upon their efforts. Christian growth is dependent upon the grace of God. We may make efforts like those of the Buddhists; however, unlike Buddhists we are not dependent upon those efforts to reach God.

Nevertheless I often wonder what really is the difference between Buddhists who through their own efforts have progressed in their path and similarly experienced Christians who, perhaps through efforts similar to those of Buddhists, have received manifold graces from God. If their spiritual experience is the same, then how are they different? The answer may be that Christians continue to be dependent upon God, whereas Buddhists, following Uchiyama Roshi, continue to believe only in their sitting. Still, should not experienced Buddhists have an intuitive perception of the existence of God when their efforts achieve a full flowering?

One of several other interesting topics Uchiyama Roshi discusses is his conviction that the Nenbutsu chant (a prayer invoking the name of the Buddha) and zazen, though rooted in different Buddhist sects offer basically the same attitude toward life.

> When we say this [the Nenbutsu chant] with our mouth, it is the Nenbutsu which expresses our deep sense of gratitude. When we perform this with our whole body, it is zazen [which expresses this

---

3.   Kosho Uchiyama Roshi, *Approach to Zen* (Tokyo: Japan Publications, 1973), 61.

attitude] . . . In other words, when people chant the Nenbutsu, they are doing zazen with their mouth, and when we do zazen, we are performing the Nenbutsu with our whole body.[4]

The roshi goes on to say that the attitude we take during zazen also determines the attitude we take toward our whole life and toward everyday activity.

This is similar to what I recall Abbot Thomas saying in several of his talks to the monks at the monastery last summer (1974). Father Thomas frequently pointed to the similarities between sitting quietly in a church, the repetition of a short prayer, and zazen. He stressed the attitude underlying all of these approaches. What is this attitude? Uchiyama Roshi answers:

> Look at the following quotes from the Bible: *"God's will be done."* *"Whether therefore you eat, or drink, or whatever you do, do all to the glory of God."* *"Because God loves us we know love. We express our love for God by loving others."* This basic Christian attitude towards life is also the basic Buddhist attitude towards life.[5]

Elsewhere he calls that attitude compassion. I doubt that Uchiyama Roshi's definition of this spiritual attitude of Zen differs markedly from Father Thomas' understanding of the spiritual attitude of Christian prayer.

Another interesting point that the roshi makes concerns the commitment to zazen and the concept of repentance. Since Uchiyama Roshi holds that "zazen is to the Buddhist what God is to the Christian,"[6] he believes it is important that the student of Zen act in accordance with the entire earth and all sentient beings. In other words, the disciple vows to do zazen until arriving at such a perspective. This is at once the course of the student's whole life and at the same time his or her direction for here and now.

Such a vow cannot help but bring frequent failures and with them a desire for repentance. True repentance, the roshi believes, is "to stand sinful before the Absolute and let the light of the Absolute shine on you."

> Simply doing zazen is itself the realization of true repentance. We who sit zazen take a vow in zazen which gives the direction to our lives, and at the same time in our acts of repentance we return to this zazen. Thus the life of repentance and the vow, watched over, guided and given strength by zazen is the Buddhist's religious life. Without the vow there would be no advancement; without repentance one

---

4. Ibid., 64-65.
5. Ibid., 79.
6. Ibid., 113.

would lose the way. The vow gives us courage; repentance crushes our conceit. Our religious life must take this kind of vivid living.[7]

All of this can be seen in a more Christian light when we reflect on the roshi's view that "zazen is to Buddhism what God is to Christianity."[8]

Though I can't quite buy such an easy parallel, I am struck by its use in explaining vows and repentance. This is the first time I've run across their explanation in Buddhist terms.

October 11, Nagoya

The pieces of the jigsaw puzzle are falling into place. My daily routine has taken shape while weekends have allowed for considerable adventuring. My day begins at six with the reading of a few Psalms (I'm still in that habit from the Vigils office at the abbey last summer). After the Psalms I do a fifty-minute sit and then go into my living room for spiritual reading. My books are not exactly spiritual, but generally they deal with Zen–Christian issues. I just put down *Approach to Zen* and now I'm in the middle of Heinrich Dumoulin's recently published *Christianity Meets Buddhism*. After reading I listen to some soft music and prepare breakfast. Then I study Japanese by listening to tapes and following in a book. This is followed by a quick run through the daily paper and off to school by quarter to nine.

After the five-minute walk, I have my seventh-grade homeroom class and proceed through the day. My classes include tenth-grade European history, eighth-grade math, seventh-grade English, and physical education for the junior and senior high schools. I am also the college guidance counselor and assistant basketball coach for this school of two hundred students. Though exhausting, these duties force me to be on my toes. I am forever scrambling to keep ahead of the brightest kids in each of these classes, while keeping an eye out for those with problems. I can't say that it is all roses, but it is stimulating and the staff is supportive.

Getting home at five I prepare my lessons for the next day and have dinner. Around eight I go into my little *zendo* (meditation hall), an unused bedroom, for a fifty-minute sit and then read some in the Gospels. I go to bed no later than ten.

---

7. Ibid., 118, 119.

8. Ibid., 113.

Weekends are wide-open affairs. Often I have gone to Kyoto to visit my folks and slowly tour the remarkable temples there. I have also used this weekend time to do some sightseeing in the Nagoya area. Unless I stay home, these days break up my routine and I am lucky if I get in any sitting on Friday evenings, Saturdays, and Sunday mornings. In Kyoto I go to the midtown church for Mass; in Nagoya, I am beginning to attend the chapel at the Catholic university downtown.

My daily routine keeps me in good shape. I suppose it could be looked upon as an academic and religious athletics. At school I've got to be in top shape in order to be effective, while in zazen I am trying to steadily condition myself so that I may be able to handle the long sittings of a sesshin. The overall residual effect is a certain intellectual sharpness, though coupled with a lot of busyness that frequently clouds my sittings. There is indeed much on my mind while at school, and this usually seeps into my zazen. Still I cling to my practice, believing that it is better not to judge the quality of the sitting. The two tempos of my day are silence and solitude in the mornings and evenings, bracketing a hectic, worldly day. Living alone and apart is the godsend. In the silences I can come back to center.

As for things specifically Catholic, I am sorry to report that I have made little headway in finding an appropriate priest for spiritual direction. I have not yet met Father Lassalle; however, I am looking forward to a trip to Tokyo at the end of this month. I hope then to meet a few of the Jesuits at Sophia University, perhaps Father Dumoulin. The rosary I use sporadically on train trips. I would certainly appreciate daily Mass and I have not yet been to confession.

... 2

The Silent Dialogue

October 12, 1974, Kyoto

Today Claudia and I went to meet Hirata Roshi, the Abbot of Tenryu-ji Temple in northern Kyoto. Our meeting was arranged by Claudia in the hope that this lithe, fifty-five-year-old Zen master might answer some of our questions concerning Zen and Christianity. Our conversation lasted two hours and took place in the roshi's private quarters. He studied philosophy in Germany before World War II and speaks fairly good German. Claudia translated for me while using her German to communicate with the roshi. The discussion ended with the sound of temple bells signaling the start of the fall sesshin.

Hirata Roshi is pessimistic about the effect of zazen on Christians. He feels that the essence of Christianity is different from the essence of Buddhism and that the lotus posture should be utilized for realizing Buddha nature while Christian prayer postures should be employed by Christians to realize Christ in themselves. Rather than deepen Christian faith, the roshi argued, zazen may well threaten it. He was especially worried about Christian monks doing zazen and went so far as to call Father Lassalle's Zen retreat house a "great adventure" in a negative sense. Though he did not entirely close the door on the beneficial aspects of zazen for Christians, the roshi clearly would rather that Christians use their own means.

Afterward, Claudia and I rehashed the talk. This question, "Does zazen deepen or threaten one's Christian faith?" has not, until now, been too disturbing for me. I have assumed that zazen deepened my faith. Still Claudia believes that there are quite a few people, both Christian and Buddhist, who are of the same opinion as Hirata Roshi. So I need to look again at the question.

October 13, Nagoya

In his book *Christianity Meets Buddhism*, Heinrich Dumoulin has the following to say on the relationship of the Catholic Church to non-Christian religions.

> In its "Dogmatic Constitution of the Church," the [Second Vatican] Council recognized the possibility of attaining salvation outside of the institutional Church and without an explicit belief in Christ (No. 16), and thus removed a longstanding barrier to interreligious relations. And the Council's "Declaration on the Relationship of the Church to Non-Christian Religions," recounts specific religious values that are characteristic of some of the great religions. Through his belief in the guidance of God, whose "saving designs extend to all men," the Christian can recognize God's saving action at work in all religions. He can, if he looks with an open heart and mind, grow to see that the Far Eastern Religions which disclose precious values of inner life, could not have emerged without some form of divine assistance. [The understanding Christian can then come to see] that the non-Christian religions contribute to the salvation of mankind, and the recognition of this may pave the way for fruitful discussion.[1]

The dialogue with non-Christian religions does not have religious unity as its goal. The establishment of a single world religion in which all existing religions would merge is emphatically not the purpose. The syncretism in such an ideal is unacceptable not only to most believers in Christianity, but also to the adherents of other religions. In his book, Father Dumoulin states that the first goal of dialogue is to gain and deepen mutual understanding and cooperation, and to recognize each other's values. But then he hastens to add that "the depth of reciprocal communication. . . will depend on the depth of the religious experience of the partners in the dialogue."[2] Without this depth, and despite sincere friendship, the scope of communication will be unavoidably limited.

Father Dumoulin points out that the dialogue can only fruitfully begin on a spiritual plane. "There can be no doubt about the common ground of all religions, but it cannot be grasped in words."[3] The claim of Christianity to absoluteness and universality is founded on the event and fact of Jesus Christ. Non-Christians do not accept this fact. And yet a Christian who would try to convince his non-Christian friend that his values were actually

---

1. Heinrich Dumoulin, *Christianity Meets Buddhism*, (LaSalle, Ill.: Open Court, 1974), 3.

2. Ibid., 36.

3. Ibid., 54.

Christian would meet not only with incomprehension but also with a deep resentment (In turn, are our Christian values actually Buddhist?). The Christian must therefore take the "otherness" of the other's religion seriously. Buddhism is not vaguely equivalent to Christianity. It is a separate religion. And yet there is a common spiritual ground.

When Hirata Roshi told Claudia and me that the essence of Christianity is different from the essence of Buddhism, he may have been simply protecting the integrity of the two religions. Each is a separate path with its own formidable doctrine and tradition, and it may have been for him threatening and demeaning to each religion for us to try to mix and match their spiritual methods.

In contrast to the roshi's stand, we who *are* Christians and are doing zazen are mixing methods at an early stage of religious experience. But we are not adopting Buddhism. My pursuit here in Japan is less centered upon Buddhism than it is upon Zen. The attitude of Zen and the posture of zazen can be, I believe, effectively severed from Buddhism.

The first time I can recall Zen being explained to me it was by Sasaki Roshi speaking to a group of Christians at Spencer. He told us that Zen can be found in all true religions. He spoke of it as a spiritual attitude that results not only from zazen but from intensive spiritual practices found in other religions. Later on I had someone explain to me that zazen was not strictly Buddhist either: before the beginning of Buddhism, when the Buddha sat for six days under the Bodhi tree and attained enlightenment, there was only zazen. The Buddhist religion evolved *after* the Buddha's enlightenment. So, strictly speaking, zazen is not Buddhist. Buddhism developed after the Buddha's enlightenment, which came through the spiritual practice of zazen.

Following this thinking, might it be that the attitude of Zen is already present in Christianity, as it is in all true religions? And might it be that the one great benefit that Zen Buddhism has over Zen in other faiths is the posture of zazen? Part of my purpose here in Japan is to see how Father Lassalle and others are trying to integrate zazen with the Christian faith. Those of us who are looking into Zen Buddhism are primarily concerned with the posture and practice of zazen. To grant credence to our actions I need only refer to the Vatican II's urging of explorations of non-Christian religions. Still, it is fair to ask, why are Christians doing zazen at all? Why not the more traditional Christian practices instead?

Answering for myself, I can only say that zazen was the first serious spiritual practice I came across and that it worked for me. I am a Catholic more because of my zazen than in spite of it. I did it before I became a

Catholic, and in a large part it was responsible for my entering the Church. The path that I have willy-nilly come to follow involves both the Christian sacraments and zazen. What results from my zazen, the spiritual experience, is present in both Christianity and Buddhism. What makes me Christian is my faith in the guidance and grace of God.

This said, I cannot abide by Hirata Roshi's hands-off warning and yet I do agree with Dumoulin that the real dialogue cannot begin on the level of dogma. My approach to Zen cannot be primarily through books but must be through religious practice. Religious experience makes it possible to establish contact, while doctrines stand in irreconcilable opposition. Because of this, spiritual practice must emerge as the central aspect in my coming to grips with the use of zazen in Christian settings.

October 23, Nagoya

Perhaps the best part of the Christian–Buddhist dialogue occurs in silence. Once words are used—and the more words the worse—the dialogue degenerates. I would like to believe that the Christian–Buddhist dialogue has been in full communion since time immemorial. In our eager quest to articulate the possibilities of such a meeting perhaps we are, ironically, pulling it apart. Any dialogue may be futile and a hindrance to a silent East–West union that is eternally present to those with enough light to become aware of it. Interest in dialogue must, in the end, point back to our personal religious practice.

Perhaps it is better to sit, better to pray, and to realize the silence that transcends dialogue, that point of realization where one knows intuitively that there is no gap between East and West, than to ask unnecessary questions. Hirata Roshi, ever on my mind these days, may have been saying just this. Better not to inquire, better to practice with what you have.

October 26, Nagoya

In my eighth-grade math class we are studying the addition and subtraction of negative numbers. I am responsible for teaching the subject, so I am trying to understand it. After a few days now I believe I grasp the use of negative numbers and so does the rest of the class. But even though I can handle the rudimentary skills of adding and subtracting negative numbers, I don't know how this body of information fits into mathematics as a whole. Not I, not my class, nor even my book can explain what exactly is the relationship of these numbers to the whole of mathematics. Yet I know that there must be a greater relationship which my limited knowledge of math is keeping me from perceiving.

There is an analogy here to my Christian way of looking at Buddhism. Buddhists, in my role or that of my students, can do the math. They can handle negative numbers: their spiritual practice is an effective means to an ineffable reality. Since they can handle negative numbers, they can score well on the test. They can arrive at an experience of God, though they may not call it that, through their Buddhist spiritual practices.

The way that a Christian goes about understanding negative numbers may be different from the way a Buddhist does—or it may be similar. The spiritual practices may differ, they may closely parallel, yet both lead to the transcendent silence. The difference between Christianity and Buddhism is not so much one of differing spiritual practices or differing experiences as it is differing explanations of that experience.

For Christians it is important that they know how negative numbers relate to the whole of mathematics. Buddhists, on the other hand, are less concerned with understanding this relationship. They are less concerned with the relationship of their spiritual experience to a larger religious framework than are Christians. The Buddhists' practice gives them results: they can add and subtract those numbers. Their spiritual experience is legitimate;they know the silence. Why then, they ask, must they know anything about the broader framework—the relationship of their experience to God?

The broader explanation of Christianity is not so much denied by Buddhism as it is deemed unnecessary, even frivolous. The Zen master will quickly evict you from *dokusan* (a private interview) once you start talking about dogma. What is *given* to Christians as dogma, is simply not mentioned in Buddhism. It remains for Buddhists with a philosophical bent to ponder the relationship of their experience to questions such as the creation of the world and its meaning. Though I frankly doubt that pondering the Trinity would greatly deepen the spiritual experience of advanced Buddhists, I think it would surely assist in their understanding of the broader context of their experience. As a Christian, I believe that the Christian explanation is broader, more satisfying, and, most importantly, true. It is the explanation that makes me a Christian, not the spiritual experience.

Δ

October 27, Nagoya

I have just returned from a trip to Sophia University in Tokyo. This school's Jesuit faculty boasts Fathers Johnston, Lassalle, and Dumoulin, priests in the forefront of the Christian–Buddhist dialogue. Father Johnston is now planting Zen–Christian seeds on a lecture tour of Australia and the United States. I will see Father Lassalle next week, but Father Dumoulin was available for a visit.

Father Dumoulin is a bouncy fellow in his seventies. He is the recognized authority on Zen Buddhism in the West as well as a practicing student of Zen meditation. Father Dumoulin believes that the Christian–Buddhist dialogue has two aspects: spiritual practice and intellectual reflection. Of the two, he emphasizes the importance of practice. He said that Zen meditation is an accomplished fact accepted by the church (the archbishop of Tokyo, among others) and pursued by hundreds of Christians in the Tokyo area. Quizzing me on my own practice, Father Dumoulin reminded me that it was important to read scripture as regularly as I sat.

As for Hirata Roshi, Dumoulin was both surprised and amused at the roshi's discouraging Claudia and me from zazen. Hirata is presently translating a book for Dumoulin into Japanese and the two are old friends. Father Dumoulin said that he respected the roshi's position but thought it a bit naïve. Christians are now doing zazen and getting results that do not threaten but rather deepen their faith.

In other brief comments, Father Dumoulin said that the religious sisters in Japan seem to be getting more easily into zazen than are the priests. The lead is being taken by the Carmelite nuns.

He also mentioned that the leader in East–West monastic ventures is a Benedictine abbot, Father Bede Griffiths, an Englishman who is experimenting with a Christian ashram in India. In Japan, Father Lassalle's Zen retreat house was the closest thing to a Zen–Christian form of monasticism of which he was aware.

A Letter from Father Thomas

November 15, Spencer

I have been away for almost a month. I was happy to receive and read the letters which arrived while I was away. Your research into Christian Zen masters and into the Japanese culture is very interesting, and I appreciate your sharing it with us.

I think your schedule is very good, considering all that you have to do. Even without daily Mass, I think you are doing very well. Sitting for Christians should be a very real spiritual communion with the Lord. I am sure it is good for you to have to mix a lot of activity with your morning and evening solitude.

I am enclosing a picture taken at your baptism. you came out especially well. I am sure your parents will be pleased to see it.

Three Retreats

November 10, 1974, Outside of Tokyo
Father Lassalle's Zen Retreat House

To get to Father Lassalle's Zen retreat house, I rode for three hours on a train from Nagoya to Tokyo, hopped a second train to the western out-skirts of the city, and a third to some mountain foothills. I then hailed a taxi as the early evening mist descended, and rode for fifteen miles along the course of an old river bed, climbing ever upward along a winding, narrow road. Gradually we seemed to pass out of modern civilization and into a land of isolated mountain valleys which have for centuries nurtured the seasonal rhythms of rural Japan.

At a final twist a black sign reached out with the words "Zen Retreat House" in white letters. Down below the sign I could hear the loud gurgle of a river. The pine walls of the nearly vertical hills enclosed the dirt trail I was about to descend.

After paying the driver, I pushed past the sign. Walking slowly down the path, the dark night camouflaged the gorge at my right and made the river sound close at hand. In a few minutes time, a soft lamplight appeared ahead revealing a small single-story complex of buildings and weaving corridors all sleek in bamboo and white.

Slipping off my shoes, I entered quietly, and cautiously walked the dark corridor toward the faint sound of conversation. Light streaked from under a door up ahead. Suddenly bursting forth in single file, teacups in hand and determination in the eyes, came fifteen Japanese men and a few foreigners. Father Oka, a redwood-like priest looking for all the world like a Zen monk, led the procession. With a slight movement he motioned for me to trail along behind. I dropped my pack, folded my hands at the chest in proper Zen manner, and succumbed to the mystery of this unearthly parade as it plunged down the darkened corridor.

I had entered into a sesshin now only a few hours old. I had entered the sesshin like a man might cut in on a woman on the dance floor, content to be with her for just a few moments of movements and smiles but no conversation and therefore much mystery. I came late and I would have to leave early. I would not speak once with any of these people who now paraded ahead of me into the dark.

The line marched on through bleakly lit corridors finally arriving at a large room with a fifteen-foot ceiling and cement floor. I noted all this later, for all I could see this first time was a colossal ROCK plunged into the middle of the room. This was the zendo, the scene for all meditation. We entered, bowing to the ROCK. Later I realized that there was a crucifix lying atop the ROCK. Crucifix or not, the ROCK emitted a presence which commanded a bow.

The room was set with *tatami* (straw) matted platforms raised two feet off the ground and extending ten feet from all walls. Zen cushions rested on these mats. I soon would be spending seven hours of my day on those cushions. After a few instructions given to all, Father Oka came to lead me to my room, cold and thoroughly Japanese. There was nothing Western in the retreat house save Christianity, and that too seemed native.

The following schedules were listed on the wall outside the zendo.

Sesshin		*Weekends (Saturday)*	
4:00–4:20 A.M.	Rise	2:00–5:00 P.M.	Arrive
4:20–5:00	Zazen	5:30–6:00	Zazen
5:00–6:00	Mass	6:00–8:00	Supper and
6:00–7:00	Breakfast and		optional zazen
	work	8:00–8:40	Zazen
7:30–8:10	Zazen	8:40–9:00	Kinhin & interval
8:10–8:30	Kinhin[1] & interval	9:00–9:40	Kinhin & bed
8:30–9:40	Lecture & interval		*(Sunday)*
9:40–10:20	Zazen (Dokusan)[2]	5:00–5:30 A.M.	Rise
10:20–10:30	Interval	5:30–6:10	Zazen

1. Walking meditaion.

2. A private interview with the teacher.

10:30–11:00	Zazen		6:10–7:00	Mass
11:00–11:30	Lunch		7:00–7:30	Breakfast
1:30–2:10	Zazen		7:30–8:30	Housework
2:10–2:30	Kinhin		8:30–9:00	Optional zazen
2:30–3:10	Zazen (dokusan)		9:00–9:40	Zazen
3:10–3:20	Interval		9:40–10:00	Kinhin & interval
3:20–3:50	Zazen		10:00–10:40	Zazen
3:50–4:30	Optional zazen		10:40–11:00	Kinhin & interval
4:30–5:00	Supper		11:00–11:30	Zazen
6:20–7:00	Zazen		11:30–12:00	Lunch
7:00–7:20	Kinhin & interval		1:30–2:00	Zazen
7:20–8:00	Zazen		2:00–2:20	Kinhin & interval
8:00–8:20	Kinhin & interval		2:20–3:10	Lecture
8:20–9:00	Zazen (tea)		3:10–3:50	Zazen
9:00	Bed		3:50–4:15	Tea, depart

Weekdays

5:00–5:30	Rise
5:30–6:10	Zazen
6:10–7:00	Mass
7:00–7:30	Breakfast
7:30–8:30	Housework
11:30–12:00	Zazen
12:00–12:30	Lunch
2:00–4:00	Work
5:30–6:00	Zazen
6:00–6:30	Supper
9:00–9:40	Zazen
10:00	Bed

After my first day at the retreat house, my enduring impression is how thoroughly this place tries to emulate the tough, disciplined, austerity of a Zen monastery. Father Lassalle plays the role of the roshi by having dokusan during zazen. Father Oka emulates a head monk and so runs the zendo as well as the daily affairs of the retreat house. Mass is celebrated on the ROCK in the zendo each morning after an hour's sit. This, coupled with the Christian spiritual counseling given by Father Lassalle in dokusan, accounts for the only spoken words aside from meal prayers. All else is silence and sitting.

The fact that Father Lassalle is a Christian missionary has to be taken into account in trying to understand the overtly Zen monastic atmosphere of his retreat house. Foreigners are welcome, but Lassalle's primary efforts are intended for Japanese Catholics. One of the major problems for converts in Japan has been the narrow views of Christian missionaries who have tended to see little of religious value in Japanese culture. Too frequently converts have been forced to adopt the overly intellectual spiritual means of Western Christianity and abandon the less foreign, more recognizable spiritual practices of their native culture. At his retreat house, Father Lassalle seems to have found a remedy. While not denying anything that is essential to Catholicism, he is trying to rescue the Japanese Catholic from this unnecessary problem by reaffirming the more native spiritual practice of Zen meditation. Father Lassalle is trying to show that zazen can be effectively employed as a spiritual practice within the universal Christian faith. Seen in this light, the overtly Zen atmosphere of the retreat house makes more sense. Father Lassalle has been encouraged in this enterprise by Yamada Roshi, the Zen master under whom he studies. He believes that he can direct others only up to his own level of spiritual development and that doing this in a roshi-like role is both a natural and effective way to help his people.

The retreatants here do an astounding amount of meditation compared to retreatants in the United States. Every day during my stay we did at least seven hours of sitting. Even so, I was told that people line up months in advance to come here and submit to this difficult grind. The attraction of freezing in November cold, eating rice gruel, and suffering through intense leg pains for two to seven days at a stretch may sound inscrutable to the Westerner, yet this appears to be the sort of retreat for which many Japanese Catholics are clamoring. It is an opportunity to plant their faith in their culture through their culture's spiritual means.

There is a bleak austerity to this place that makes it close to unbearable at the outset, but after packing away a few hours of zazen the place has become a stark black-and-white wonderland, a terribly beautiful mountain valley, with crisp air, an enchanted land. My problem so far is less with the long hours of sitting than the lack of heat,—it is freezing—and the poor rice gruel meals. Perhaps I am soft, but I fail to see the spiritual benefit one derives from enduring the latter two.

Still, thinking again of the retreat house situation in the States, could it be that retreat leaders have wrongly developed a low level of expectation for their retreatants? What if such a rigorous regime were made available to laypeople in the United States? Would there be a flood of interest? Has anyone tried? It would not have to be zazen, just severe. It might be a smashing success and found to be desperately needed.

In my first dokusan with Father Lassalle, I asked how the Catholic rite of confession fit in with zazen. I had not been to my first confession since baptism in August three months ago. Father Lassalle said that zazen and confession are not interchangeable. Though the need for confession may be assuaged by zazen, he said that confession was still something special and that I should do it as well. I understood this to mean that zazen might be something like an informal form of confession, but that I needed absolution to complete my repentance. I accepted this and said that I would like to confess at my next dokusan. Father Lassalle nodded.

I gave my first confession in dokusan the next day. Answering the gong that signaled these interviews in the midst of a sitting, I rose from my place in the zendo, quietly walked down the bamboo corridor, ducking the low ceiling beams, and arrived at the waiting room, bowing to my predecessors in line. When my turn came I answered the bell from Father Lassalle's room with a bell of my own, mounted the stairs, bowed to a Japanese nun as she passed, reached the top and entered the small dokusan room, something like a confessional, with a bow. I continued with the series of bows afforded a Zen master, until I was sitting knee to knee in front of Lassalle. Erect in formal lotus posture and rich, black robes, Father Lassalle listened to my confession. Then bowing my head while he spread his arms, I listened as he gave me absolution in Latin. Christian absolution in Latin tongue from a German priest in a Zen retreat house in the mountains of Japan. My first confession.

November 12, Nagoya

Trying to "find myself" in a college psychology course is different from trying to find myself in my generation, and that in turn is different from the search to find myself in all of humanity. Yet each leads to the next deeper turn in the seeking and nowhere does there appear to be an end. It is a perennial lost-and-found in which at no time am I fully certain that I am completely found yet neither am I wholly lost. I have no fully known position for I am forever moving to the next.

I am certain about my continuing uncertainty. I cannot describe where I stand. Still, however amorphous my life may appear, it is rooted in God and zazen. My practices of Gospel reading and zazen order my life and without them I am secular—lost to divine direction. This is a solace but not an endpoint. Things make sense and occur as they should when my spiritual life is in shape, but never can I be fully sure what is to happen next.

I find it difficult to speculate about my future. Rather than wonder, I burrow into my zazen and my solitude. I wait. Also, I am so wrapped up in these spiritual questions that I do not have time for pursuing possible relationships with women. And I have difficulty talking, really talking, with anyone other than those who are doing as I am. This is not so wonderful for I have yet to resolve so many things. The simple questions of human affection, of marriage, questions as to what really are my fundamental, undeniable human needs are yet to be answered. They gnaw at me. I wish to weigh and measure everything and take no false steps. I am not so much troubled as I am anxious. I have my practice, but what of my life?

November 20, Nagoya

Recently I met an interesting Japanese priest, Father Okumura. We talked together in a small, cozy room at his church in downtown Nagoya. Father Okumura was an ardent Zen Buddhist layman studying under Nakagawa-Soen Roshi, who is now in New York City, when he first ran across the Bible. After a period of study and reflection, Okumura told his roshi that he was very much interested in Christianity. Nakagawa-Soen responded by suggesting he be baptized. Soon afterward Father Okumura entered the church and later the Carmelite Order, doing his seminary work in France. Today Okumura is principally occupied teaching theology at the Catholic university here in Nagoya, giving retreats, and serving in two churches—one here, the other in Kyoto. He is also a leading advocate of a Japanese Catholic theology. From what I gathered, this now involves developing accurate Japanese translations of Catholic terms. In addition, he has just published a book on prayer in which he contributes toward a Japanese understanding of prayer.

We touched briefly on several topics. In discussing my interview with Hirata Roshi, Father Okumura thought that the roshi had been trying to shock me into an awareness of the present moment in telling me not to do zazen, rather than trying to redefine my spiritual practice. In reference to Father Lassalle's retreat house, Okumura said that Lassalle received vital help in planning that place from a Japanese Catholic layman who had been a Zen monk for more than ten years before his conversion.

About Father Oka, Lassalle's right hand man, he is a Jesuit who succeeded in getting permission from his superior to stay at Lassalle's retreat house. Father Okumura said that he supported Lassalle's efforts, but he hoped for the day when a place like Lassalle's would not have to so strictly follow the Zen monastic model. He sees zazen as one of many methods and not as a tool of the overwhelming importance that Father Lassalle tends to attach to it. To be sure, Father Okumura does two hours of prayer each day in Zen posture. Still he is not so completely an advocate of zazen that he eschews other methods.

Father Okumura's chief concern is the theological instruction of Japanese Catholics. The overt signs of Christianity (churches, crosses and the like), ever-present in the West, are not so ubiquitous here. Therefore he wants to keep the theology of Christianity always in the minds of his students and retreatants. Father Lassalle, on the other hand, works on the more strictly experiential end of things.

Our talk ended on an intriguing note when Okumura urged me to see Father Oshida, a Dominican living in a rural mountain community and doing zazen.

During the week after Christmas I am planning to go up to Hokkaido (Japan's northernmost island) to visit the Trappists living in Hakodate. The abbot, Father Bonaventure, answered my letter asking to visit and said that I would be welcome. After this trip I plan to take another before too long to visit Father Oshida's community.

A Letter from Father Thomas

November 15, Spencer

I am glad Father Lassalle straightened you out about confession, at least for the present. It is true, you may feel closer to God during zazen, but do not forget the Zen principle that it is by *doing* something that you actually gain enlightenment. The sacraments are marvelous ways of gaining an awareness of what we already have through baptism or, if we already have this awareness, of increasing it or of expressing it. Thus, in confessing our sins, we receive an ever deepening awareness that we have been forgiven and indeed possess God's infinite forgiveness. In the Eucharist, Christ approaches us from without, but he is also waiting for us within. In the Eucharist both become one. True interior silence is manifested in action.

Δ

A Letter from Brother Anselm

December 16, Spencer

Thanks very much for your very interesting letters—especially the telling of your visit to Father Lassalle's place. It has certainly been very interesting and encouraging for me.

Our winter austerity heating program has forced us out of the chapter room "zendo." We are using the north aisle of the abbey church. I, however, have repaired to a spare room in the lower dorm. All, however, goes well as far as I can see. I am very carefully reading *Approach to Zen* by Uchiyama Roshi and, while not understanding all he says, am profiting from it. Thanks for sending it. I am also finding many "Zen" resonances in the Gospel according to St. John, especially where I am reading now—fourteenth and fifteenth chapters.

I hope all continues well for you and that we all grow together in our respective searches through the power of Jesus who *"sits at the right hand of the Father."*

Δ

A Letter from Brother Aidan

December 23, Spencer

Your letters are something of a vicarious pilgrimage for me and, as with all my contact with the East, they give me new and great faith in my own tradition. You must blaze your own trail and I must forge ahead on my old mountain road with many sudden turns. You don't know what God wants you to do so you wait. I came to the monastery because I knew and I stay because I know what he wants. But, now that I'm here what do I do? Wait.

The Epiphany is almost upon us. This is the feast of the East. *"Surge illuminare. . ."*—arise, be enlightened. This idea comes back again and again in the classical liturgy of these days. Did the Magi "know" who this Child was? Were they enlightened? If so, how?

Perhaps you could bring up this question to those with whom you are speaking: "What is the place of grace in Christian Zen?" For me this is a great problem on the intellectual plane and contributes much to my doubts about Zen for Christians.

January 3, 1975, Nagoya
The Trappist Monastery in Hokkaido

Pluralism at the Spencer monastery is a three-ring circus when compared to the uniform monastic life at the Our Lady of Phare Trappist monastery in Hakodate on Japan's northernmost island of Hokkaido. Each monastery seems to reflect in some measure the spiritual life of its broader culture. This metaphor of a circus may help explain why Abbot Bonaventure, whom I have been visiting this week, considers, in a very positive way, the Spencer Trappists' interpretations of pluralism to be "entertaining." What with Eastern Orthodox, Zen, Yoga, Transcendental Meditation, and other practices all in use to some degree at Spencer, the American Trappists seem to retain a spirit of diversity that is absent in Japanese culture and in Japanese Trappist monasticism.

In explaining the minimal interest in zazen at his monastery, Father Bonaventure began by dividing his forty monks into two groups. Half of them come from old Japanese Catholic families in Nagasaki, a port city in southern Japan. The Nagasaki area is famous to Japanese Catholics as the focus of hundreds of years of missionary work. It is also infamous for its equally long history of persecutions, often spearheaded by the local Buddhist establishment. About half of the monks at the Hokkaido monastery are therefore from Catholic families with fresh memories of Buddhist persecution. The other half are converts, proselytized at a time when Buddhism was denounced as a black, idolatrous religion by Catholic missionaries. Consequently there is not a great deal of interest in zazen and what interest there is is handled delicately.

The few monks who do practice zazen are young men who entered this monastery after the reforms of Vatican II. One of them, a graduate of a Buddhist university, has a grandfather who was in Zen training before converting to Catholicism. Given the religious background of these Japanese Trappists, it does not seem likely that this monastery will soon favor zazen as a spiritual practice. Still, there is some interest and it is not discouraged by the abbot.

Abbot Bonaventure is a wonderful man who is going out of his way to spend time with me. He is the only multilingual contact for foreign visitors, having learned English to pass the time when bedridden two years ago. He apparently knows French as well. Unfortunately his excellent language skills afford him the added burden of dealing with guests as well as the many monks for whom he is spiritual father.

Our Lady of Phare is perched on a rise overlooking the ocean with a mountain at its back. The primary source of revenue is dairy farming, though there are also two cottage industries, butter and cookies. Because of the workload, the times for communal prayer are a bit compressed at the beginning and end of each work day. The schedule is as follows:

3:45 A.M.	Vigils	8:15	Sext, work
5:00	Lauds	11:30	Lunch (guests)
5:30	Meditation in the church	1:10	None, work
5:45	Mass	5:30	Dinner (guests)
6:30	Tierce	7:15	Vespers & Compline
7:00	Breakfast (guests)	8:00	Bed

The brothers here share Spencer's penchant for an imaginative variety of work buildings, each creatively nooked and crannied to particular tastes. And yet there are a number of things here you will not find at Spencer. These include: the Japanese deep bath tubs, *ofuro*, which require that you clean yourself before entering their steamy waters; picture frames hung all along one side of the main cloister corridor, each one proclaiming a line or two from the Gospels in black and white Japanese (this type of exhortation I have only seen before in Zen temples); finally, certainly the coming fashion for all you Zen Trappist fans, a small tatami-matted room in austere Zen style where the few who are interested in zazen do their sitting.

Whenever I do a retreat among Trappist monks, I find myself comparing the way I lead my life with the Trappist way. On this retreat I noticed again my weakness. All people are weak, but monks seem to know this better than most. In my efforts to do zazen and read the Gospels, I am running up against my own lethargy. It was easier to do these things a few months ago when I was living in the Spencer monastery and harder now that my life has established a routine outside of monastic supports. For all my pious intentions, I am finding it difficult to keep to my daily sitting practice. Either I sit for shorter times, miss a sitting, or perhaps excuse myself from Bible reading. Whatever the corner-cutting may be, I am now witnessing an inexorable recession from my conviction to sit and read as planned. I am learning, again, that I cannot do it all myself and that I need some sort of buttressing in order to follow through on my daily practice. This is the toughest lesson. The nature and degree of my buttressing is the central issue. I ask, How weak am I? Would daily Mass, if it were available, be enough? Perhaps a week's retreat every three months? Every summer at a monastery? How much support do I need? It is easy to say that I will inevitably become a monk, but I would rather not jump that far just yet. Better I learn by my own slow, frustrating experience just where God intends me to be.

I have also been thinking about the problem of integrating foreign religions with alien cultures. This Hokkaido monastery is, for me, too imitative of Western monasteries (Someone at Spencer warned me that walking into Our Lady of Phare would be like walking into a monastery in France). In the United States, two years ago, I witnessed the reverse situation when I visited Sasaki Roshi's Zen Center in southern California. There the roshi was trying to juxtapose Zen monastic life with American culture. Each of these attempts to integrate foreign religions with an alien culture has begun with a stark juxtaposition of the two. That is, a European monastery in Japan, a Zen monastery in southern California. This may be a necessary initial stage as a religion adapts to a new culture (Father Lassalle's Zen retreat house is a variation on this stage. In his case the new religion has perhaps become too imitative of the native culture). I wonder what will be the next stage. How long will it be until the odd contrasts evolve to form integrated wholes?

Sasaki Roshi provided an answer when he spoke at Spencer a while ago. Then he said that it would take perhaps fifty to one hundred years before Zen Buddhism could be absorbed into American culture. He did not predict the form it would have to take to survive, but I remember several of the monks speculating that zazen might ultimately abide in the belly of the Catholic Church. Wild speculation.

I asked Abbot Bonaventure what he thought, not of Zen Buddhism's future in the States, but the future of his own Christian monasticism in the midst of Japanese culture. He responded saying that the integration of Japanese culture and Christian religion might take another three hundred years. Buddhism took even longer in Japan. By pushing the integration of Christianity and Japanese culture, Christian missionaries may achieve an institutional integration of sorts, but they will surely not succeed in imbuing the culture with a Christian spirit. Father Bonaventure believes that there has to be a more fully developed Christian spirituality among the Christians now converted in Japan before we can ever consider a broad-based integration of Christianity and Japanese culture. This will take time, he says, and we must be patient.

Δ

February 9, Kyoto

I am at a coffee shop outside the gates of Daitoku-ji in northern Kyoto. This morning I left my parents' house to come here and spend the day walking about the meticulous gardens of this famous Zen monastery.

After an initial flurry of contacts, I have reached a watershed in my journey both here and in life. There is too much undigested material that needs attention before I can proceed. Not only what I am learning about Zen, but also my whole progression since first encountering the monastery and converting to Catholicism, needs to be better understood and integrated into my life. My daily practice proceeds normally. At times I am less interested in the East–West conversation than I am in listening to the Spirit in my daily life. Sometimes I think it might have been better for me to go to France rather than Asia, to sink myself neck-deep in the church. But here I am, and though I miss the ubiquity of the local parish, it is all right. I am sitting for about two hours a day and I am not reading much outside of the Gospels, *The Imitation of Christ*, and the *Cloud of Unknowing*.[3]

Father Thomas, I need some advice. "Lord Have Mercy," which I repeat in zazen each day, has begun to wear on me. It is not so much the meaning as it is the words. I would rather utter syllables or sounds than words. Could you suggest a short, perhaps Latin, alternative?

A Letter from Father Thomas

March 8, Spencer

You asked about an alternative to the Jesus Prayer or the part of it which you repeat during zazen. I do not know that the words or syllables are so important as the intention you have in entering zazen as an expression of your Christian faith. In the book you so kindly sent us, called *Approach to Zen*, Uchiyama Roshi recommended, as I remember, just returning existentially to one's position or reaffirming one's position in zazen as the principal means of "not going with" thoughts as they rise up in the mind.

Along with this idea I would like to add a few thoughts provided by Roshi Sasaki in advising us as Christian monks. He said,

---

3. Thomas à Kempis, *The Imitation of Christ* (New York: Harper and Row, 1970); *The Cloud of Unknowing and the Book of Privy Counseling*, ed. William Johnston (New York: Doubleday, 1973). The latter is a fourteenth-century text attributed to an unidentified Carthusian or Cistercian monk.

"Do your meditation in the context of contemplating the cross. The cross is the symbol of the perfect unification of all existence. You are one with Jesus on the cross in perfect unity in meditation. When I make the sign of the cross, I embrace the entire universe." At another time he said, "Just as christ took all the sins of the world upon himself, and all pain, so in meditation we do the same. How should a christian approach Zen meditation? You should find yourself on the cross in perfect unity with Christ. There is no need to take the cross to yourself as an object. You are already on it as a Christian. On the cross one is in the state of union."

I would like now to try to put these two approaches together and out of that insight suggest a few words that you might use in zazen.

To sit in zazen is an expression of the reality of your inmost being as a man in whom Jesus Christ is present on the cross and risen. It is a marvelous way of identifying yourself with that interior reality. In zazen you sit down on the cross with Jesus and identify with his willingness to die on the cross, i.e., you affirm your determination to die to the ego-self so that you can live the risen life of Jesus which has already been given you, but which is still secret because of the life of the ego. To sit is to allow the life of Christ to rise up quietly within you. Thus the very position itself is an affirmation of your willingness to be on the cross with Christ, to share his dying, which was really a death for you, and to wait for his resurrection within you.

This is an insight which is difficult enough to articulate. Maybe some of it will have meaning for you. The words I was thinking of in Latin are from Paul, "*Cum Christo crucifixus sum!*" The first two words would be enough after the whole idea has sunk in a little bit. The whole passage of Paul reads, "With Christ I am nailed to the cross and live, now not I, but Christ lives in me." What Zen calls the Self of one's own true nature corresponds to what Paul calls the Spirit of the inner man as opposed to the outer man, which is not only the body, but the emotions and thoughts which all go to build up what we call the ego.

I am glad you have a little breather to reflect on and assimilate all your experiences. The coming Holy Week and Easter is the time to renew your baptismal experience. You were signed over and over with the cross; when the water was poured over you, your spirit was truly enlightened. But in order to experience the resurrection, the ego must truly die. Sitting is an outward expression of your interior crucifixion—and resurrection.

Δ

March 2, Nagoya

A friend of mine who photographed for Time–Life in Vietnam has just left after staying with me for five days. His stories laid to rest any last vestiges of adventure that I may still have associated with war. He had been wounded and lived with the Viet Cong. He saved lives and his life was saved by others. On both sides he found kindness mixed with hatred and horror. No one really knew why they were there and no one wanted to be there.

Walking home one evening in Saigon, he saw eight little boys, sleeping on newspapers in the street, who asked him for food. He fed them and the next day there were forty more. Photographing for a story on orphanages in Saigon, he found that there were 400,000 orphans with only three government representatives assigned to them. Nothing made sense while everywhere the human condition, body and mind, was ripped open and bleeding.

My friend was asked by *Time* magazine to take pictures of peace for a cover story on the Kissinger treaty of late January 1973. The assignment was absurd. The editors wanted a picture of a farmer tilling in a bombed-out crater. My friend told them that there is nothing but clay for topsoil in those craters, so convulsed are they by the bombs. They asked him for a picture of a Vietnamese and some doves, he told them that the Vietnamese *eat* doves. As a result that January issue does not bear a picture of peace in Vietnam, yet the prose is of peace. The editorial board wanted it that way, though my friend pleaded that no peace was to be found.

March 2, Takamori
Father Oshida's Community

By train I traveled four hours north of Nagoya into the mountainous, wintry Japan Alps. Father Oshida's community is tucked away high in these mountains of central Japan. He wrote that I could come to visit whenever I wanted and stay as long as I would like. I went for a weekend.

Through conversations with Father Merv, an American visiting the community for a year on "prayer leave" from his diocese, I pieced together some parts of Oshida's story. He had been ordained at the age of forty after a twenty-year experience that included education in chemistry at the prestigious Tokyo University, an injury during World War II that led to a severe lung ailment, and training at a Dominican seminary in Canada. After several years of parish work in Tokyo, Father Oshida had been troubled by his war injury and had gone to a hospital in the Japan Alps for prolonged treatment and convalescence. A city boy from a Buddhist family whose father did zazen regularly, Father Oshida felt called to "the manifestations of God in the land, "as he later told me, and chose to spend a year of his convalescence living in an old, decaying Buddhist temple in one of the villages near the hospital. Stories began to circulate about this Japanese Catholic priest living as a hermit in a single-room village temple. They reached legendary proportions when he decided not to return to Tokyo but stay out in the rural village and farm. Oshida was given some land by the town fathers and began to live a primitive agrarian life. Soon others joined him: Buddhists, Catholics, men and women. They did zazen for two hours a day and held sesshin once a month. This evolving community gradually came to escape the classification system of the Dominicans and, when Father Oshida refused to alter his ways, he was nearly evicted from the order. Today Oshida explains that Father Lassalle in Tokyo was able to keep his Zen retreat house and remain in the good graces of the Jesuit order because he could explain to his superior that what he had was simply a retreat house, a recognizable institution. But Oshida had neither monastery nor retreat house, neither parish nor a convalescent home—yet a little of each.

He never did return to parish work and over the years, the last six of eleven, the Dominicans have come to tolerate him though they can't seem to understand what he is up to. The man has no plans. The door of his community is open to any and all to stay as long as they wish. He merely tries to respond to the needs of those who seek him and from such responses evolve his daily actions. The place is truly primitive and contemplative in tone.

On first glance Oshida's community is poor, though not markedly worse off than any other small farm in the area. Eight matchbox huts and houses provide shelter for hermits, retreatants, permanent members, animals, zendo, church, and eating room. No house is larger than twenty square feet and most no bigger than a large chicken coop. It is a cozy, primitive, peasant farm open to all and deeply committed to contemplation. As a westerner I imagine I am more aware of the lack of central heating, the rice diet, sitting on the floor, the language, yet too there are the elements that transcend culture—the exuberance, solidity, and contemplative mood exuded by so many here, and particularly by Father Oshida.

There are informal branches of Takamori (the name for the nearby town, but also the informal name for Oshida's community) north of the farm and in Japan's southernmost island of Kyushu. The former has only two permanent members; the latter numbers two Spanish hermits and is closed to outsiders. These Spaniards are Benedictines who tried hermit life in the Holy Land only to become tourist attractions. In Japan they seem to have found a people understanding and supportive of their needs. Indeed, Oshida's Takamori can only exist through such understanding. In the farm, in zazen, in the rural peasant life, Oshida and his community have planted Christ deep in the soil of rural Japan. And yet the community places no value on stability as such, it has no institutional roots. The foundations of the community lie more in an unbounded willingness to serve the needs of those to come. In the winter few come, and in the summer perhaps twenty at peak.

Japan has little central heating. Winter warmth is grudgingly supplied from small kerosene heaters or from hot coals placed in dug-out holes in the floor beneath the eating table. I arrived in the evening and that night there were only thick blankets piled high to keep me warm. In the morning I awoke to a six o'clock gong, dressed, and walked outside to the community's pump to brush my teeth. The ground was frozen and the air icy clear, mountains all around. I had on three layers of clothing and still I was quite cold.

At six-thirty, ten of us climbed a small rise to the small church to sit in zazen around a wooden plank on the floor that served as an altar. The woman to my left started an open fire in an iron kettle in front of her and soon smoke and warmth began to fill the room. My folded hands began to warm. We sat in silence for forty minutes, the fire crackling and smoke in our eyes. The Mass began with Oshida putting on his vestments. Everyone stayed in zazen posture. The rite took over an hour, with Father Oshida taking long pauses and proceeding with a slow, solemn sanctity. As the communion bread and wine were passed around, Oshida sang a quiet, mournful hymn while the kettle fire slowly died. After Mass we read from the Bible and adjourned.

Breakfast began at eight-thirty. We had coffee or tea and toast while sitting around a long table on the tatami floor, our feet thrust under and near the hot coals in the ground below. Other people around the table included the former head of a Dominican group of nuns who had left her order to be with this community (she is middle-aged and the domestic chief); a strong young man who serves as the straw boss for farm chores; several sisters; a young woman, and a young man. Each week the peripheral population changes, says Father Merv, but the change is never enough to alter the community's contemplative tone.

After breakfast there was a half-hour of Bible study in which Father Oshida, talking slowly and clearly, studied aloud in Japanese and English a passage or two. Following this, he and I went out to dig a ditch, do some carpentry, and carry wood. Lunch was at twelve-thirty, and then a rest period before going back to work. At four a sister came to me and I accompanied her to the wood stove and water-pump kitchen where we prepared dinner.

At five a bell sounded and we headed back to the chapel for Vespers. All of us sat in zazen for forty minutes, while the night fell and shadows began to form. Soon the kettle fire was begun and we were alone with its crackling. Time passed. The fire died and candles were passed around. Together we read some Psalms. A long pause, then Father Oshida intoned the "Salve Regina,"[4] sung quietly by six voices in the evening candlelight. A wonderful moment. Later we walked down the hill to dinner, mountain landscapes lit by moonlight shining all around us. That evening after dinner we sat around and sang Latin chants from a Dominican book used on the days before Easter. Over and over, huddled together with little light, we sang chants that came back to me hours after their singing.

I could not help but feel attached to this community after only two days. At Sunday noon I left, and the whole community followed me out to the road, waving exuberantly as I backpeddled out of sight. I am sure there was a lot that I did not see on this first visit, but I saw enough to promise myself to head back soon.

---

4. An evening hymn to the Virgin Mary.

... 4
Second Looks

Lately I have been less interested in intellectual arguments. Since leaving school I seem to have gone through a sort of intellectual disarmament from the kind of academic conversations I used to enjoy. I tend to stumble through such conversations and even apologize for a lifestyle that is more withdrawn from "worldly" affairs.

None of this really bothers me. In fact I am surprised at how much it does not bother me. It seems that as long as I do my sitting, read the Bible, and feel at peace with God, I have no reason to be upset. This sort of silent, withdrawn contentment is not the stuff needed for a good high school teacher. I have difficulty entering with abandon the "wonderful world of ideas." I lack enthusiasm. This last weekend I was at Father Oshida's community and did not want to return. I felt that the former environment was where I was intended to be.

Of late my zazen has been like a trip through a mirror. I have felt myself enter into meditation so nakedly, with such feelings of abandonment that I am both unnerved and thrilled. When I depart from this active inaction, it is as if I have reassumed a weight, the weight of the ego. It is this desire not to return to distraction, to ego, that most compels me to solitude. Yet I feel it is too early to take that greater leap. I shall probably wait until there is no leap at all—when a contemplative vocation is no longer a choice but the obvious, unavoidable next step. God's hand is leading me, I feel sure of it.

Well, Father, I hope that you and the brothers have a joyous Easter over there on your hill. I have taken to playing Brother Norbert's Compline recording at night before retiring, and every night I sing the *"Salve Regina"* with you.

A Letter from Father Thomas

March 27, Spencer

I am glad that your feelings of abandonment are growing, A contemplative vocation, whatever its specifics may eventually turn out to be as regards place or method, is a call into the unknown, like Abraham leaving his home and country in obedience to the mysterious call of God. But this movement ever beyond where we are is, of course, not so much a question of place . . .

Δ

March 20, Nagoya

Looking around my apartment this evening, I notice that everything is sadly normal. My kitchen floor splattered with grease stains near the stove, some "cleaned" dishes still betraying signs of food, the shirts in my makeshift laundry a bit too starchy for comfort, and quite a bit of dust in the hallway. I am bothered by my messy habits. For some time now I have excused myself for infractions of the "good housekeeping" practices by claiming that neatness is not in my nature. In addition to neatness problems, I also have trouble with mechanical maintenance. I am not good with my hands. I tend to write this problem off to nature as well. Perhaps this is not the answer and really the problem is laziness. Fine, but why then this anguish in me whenever I attempt to come to grips with either of these two problems?

I have read that I should try to find God in everything that I do, but do I have the right to choose the doings through which I seek to find God? I can conclude easily enough that God is in everything, yet are there some things toward which a less than meticulous, mechanically inept person like me should naturally find attraction and others from which I should be repelled? Or is it better for me to force myself to keep an immaculate household and fix my machines, though I may hate doing it every step of the way, in order to discover the peace inherent in that work? To say it another way, do I trust myself enough to know when a certain activity will not be profitable in reaching God; or, do I so distrust myself that I plunge headlong into every activity seeking the God that must be there?

At a Trappist monastery, you do not find monks who do only one specific job and are incapable of doing other jobs. However, you do find that each monk has certain gifts that lead to his doing a job that best suits those gifts. There seems to be a loosely defined area where each monk is most effective. Is this also the area in which God intended that person to work? Or is it something more fundamental, perhaps the attitude with which the monk does his work is more important than the kind of work he does?

Do we limit ourselves by acknowledging that we are not suited for certain kinds of work? Would it be harmful for the scholar to fix the pick-up truck, or would it be a tremendous opportunity for growth? The answer evades me and I feel that I am not approaching the issue properly. There is an easy answer here, something to do with distinguishing God's will from self-will.

I have rationalized for some time that I would really work on my housekeeping chores only if I felt them to obscure my relationship with God. But these things have been no great cause of remorse. I feel little guilt over dust in my hallway. Should I? Everyone who comes by to visit implies that I should. Perhaps then the cleaning that is needed should be done for others who visit here and not for me. All right, I can write my lack of housekeeping *élan* off to laziness and a lack of consideration for others. Now I am left with the problem of poor mechanical aptitude about which I feel neither pangs of remorse nor the urge to develop a mechanical mind. Should I? If I had to fix my car, I would learn how and I think I could. However, if I do not have to, if someone else can do it for me, is it right for me to let someone else do it? Do I assume that everything put before me is a task from God and intended for me to do, or do I pick and choose what tasks I will do?

In a technological society where so much is done for me, what things must I insist on doing myself? Is it only an attitude that I can choose, or should I do everything myself? And since God is ultimately directing all that I do, how can I be sure that I am following His will? The answer lies in prayer and openness certainly, and the overwhelming sense of vague darkness and mystery that I confront in trying to follow his will.

Enough of this.

Easter, 1975, Outside of Tokyo
Easter Week at Father Lassalle's Retreat House, Maundy Thursday

In a recent letter, Father Lassalle told me that the latest sesshin would have ended by the time I arrived at the retreat house for Easter week and that everyone, including himself, would have left. Still he told me to make myself at home and others would be along soon. Arriving at such an auspicious place with nothing but long, darkened corridors to greet me was disconcerting; but now, two days after my arrival, I have made myself at home.

These two days alone have been wonderful. I've been following a cycle of three sittings, a meal, read a bit by the stove (no central heating), a walk, then back to sitting. The floors in the hall creak loudly, so when I walk about from zendo to kitchen to the library to my room, I can sing as I walk and the floor creaks keep the beat. With no one here you can just imagine the scene at nine-thirty last night when I rose from the last sit and headed for coffee in the kitchen. Deep from this forgotten gorge came my bellow of the Trappist's Compline office. This is Japan? I've been having a good time.

A German lady, Mrs. Anschultz, came this morning and joined me in my rounds. She speaks some English, so during the time around the stove, we spoke a bit about Father Lassalle's doings in Germany. It was not surprising to learn that Father Lassalle is the "apostle of Zen to the Germans." Mrs. Anschultz, a Catholic, came to Zen through Transcendental Meditation and with seven years of sitting behind her she is one of Father Lassalle's earliest followers. She told me that he commands a great deal of respect in Germany. When Lassalle gives sesshin there, they are usually oversubscribed. These sesshin are given in several monastic houses with participants coming from the sponsoring house plus lay people. He gives two introductory courses, one for five days and the other for eight. Mrs. Anschultz knows quite a few contemplatives, men and women, who are finding it easier to practice Zen as part of their Christian contemplation due to Father Lassalle's efforts. Lassalle will be leaving Japan in early August for six months in Germany. There he will supervise the founding of a Zen retreat house which will be under the direction of a priest trained here by Lassalle. Father Lassalle is 76 years old and going strong.

This afternoon, Lassalle arrived and he, Mrs. Anschultz, and I held Maundy Thursday Mass at seven-thirty in the newly constructed chapel. The chapel is in a large tatami room where two monolithic rocks have been tastefully placed, surrounded by small alleys of white pebbles. The tabernacle is a hole, with an iron door, wrought in the vertical stone. The altar is the flat top of the more horizontal rock. After Mass (so good to hear it in English again—Father could have said it in German or Japanese but he said it in English for me), we paraded the Blessed Sacrament out of the chapel and down a long corridor to a small reception room. We then sat with the Sacrament before retiring.

Good Friday

This morning Father Lassalle woke me at five. We sat with the Sacrament in the reception room for forty minutes. Later, we became wholly occupied with a group of thirty-five German tourists on a whistle-stop tour of Japan. All of a sudden I became staff and set to guiding the visitors around. By evening, we had become a small group of eight. Father Oka, two young men, and two sisters had arrived. The cook has been in and out. I had a chance to speak with Father Oka in my poor Japanese while we were both on our hands and knees cleaning the kitchen floor. He is a much less rigid fellow than his behavior as disciplinarian in the zendo had led me to believe. He and Lassalle led a long Good Friday service in the chapel. Father Lassalle then clamped on a rule of silence until Saturday's midnight Mass.

Holy Saturday

It seems as if I've spent the whole day climbing around the mountains looking for flowers. Though I searched for two hours, I couldn't find any. It is early spring and only greens and buds abound. I took them back to Father Oka and he sympathized, but then told me to go out and bring back some "trees." I supposed that he meant branches, yet when I returned it was apparent that I had gotten the wrong thing. So Oka himself went out and in three minutes came back with a wonderfully gnarled old log with two budding branches. The log has become the chief decoration piece for the chapel. It fits right in with the tabernacle and the altar.

The schedule today has been ad hoc. We rose at five-thirty and did a round of zazen at six. This was followed by breakfast, zazen at nine and eleven, lunch, and free time. At three we assembled to prepare for Easter Mass. Mrs. Anschultz carved a 1975 on the candle, the sisters painted eggs, and I looked for flowers. This evening the Mass had readings in English, German, and Japanese to accommodate all. Later we had a party until three A.M. I leave for Nagoya at six-thirty this morning.

Aside from Easter, two things had my attention this week. First was my experience with poor sitting posture. On my third day I discovered a strain in the muscle that lies close to the spine in the top left portion of my back.

At the time I didn't have any explanation for this strain. On the fourth day Father Oka was in the zendo and came by to straighten my posture. Stopping behind me, Oka lightly pressed my right arm so that my body was pushed slightly to the right. This change of position made me feel very much ajar, or so I thought. In the next few minutes I slowly righted my position and wrote off Oka's correction as an oversight on his part. However, on two subsequent occasions he corrected my posture in a similar manner. Only after the third correction was I able to make the connection between my strained back muscle and Oka's posture corrections. Perhaps I *was* sitting ajar. Still the corrected posture made me feel like I was sitting at an awkward angle. I am still trying to get used to this new position.

The second thing I noticed this week was the effect of vocal exhortations in the zendo. Father Oka is the zendo's *jikijitsu* (disciplinarian). His responsibility is to allow for a deepening contemplative state to come about by encouraging meditators to make ever greater efforts. In line with this he straightens postures and uses the jikijitsu's long, thin wooden stick (*kyosaku*) to lightly rap the shoulders of meditators to alert them to a deeper awareness of God. Just before Father Oka goes on his walk around the zendo he says a few sentences. In tone these are frightening, deadly serious words which, though spoken in Japanese, never fail to send chills of apprehension up my spine. All that Oka is trying to do, though, is shake us all into an attentive frame of mind. He seems to be sternly addressing the devil of distraction that nags us all during meditation. His words cut right through the zazen silence and shake me to the quick. They force a greater intensity out of me which, in more lax moments, I had doubted was there. As a result of these admonitions, Oka appears to be a somberly intense man, but really all he is doing is what zendo disciplinarians have been doing for centuries, trying to help meditators deepen their awareness. Isn't this too the ultimate task of every Catholic priest?

One last note. Father Lassalle encouraged me to do longer three-to-four-hour sits on my own, perhaps on a biweekly or monthly basis. Particularly on days when I can not get to Sunday Mass. Though without a roshi, such mini-sesshin, he suggested, might be helpful in deepening my daily practice.

A Letter from Father Edward John

April 18, Spencer

It has been a very cold spring. We just last week moved from Father Joseph's office to the chapter room for morning zazen. We have a nice little group at present, seven of us: Anselm, Freddie, myself, and four novices. There is also a pheasant outside who starts squawking just as we start sitting. Maybe the same one who was here for our last sesshin—do you recall? Actually I enjoy the squawk of a pheasant.

It is interesting how much my own recent experiences with zazen parallel yours. Even before you mentioned it, I was working on the lotus position. It is obviously going to take some time—for me at least. I had just begun too, to pay more attention to posture in general. No wobbling, head back, and so forth. I think this is a great value, maybe the greatest, of sitting with others. More than all the particulars though, I think just sitting day by day, and reading the Bible, is the Way. This ongoing discipline makes personal fulfillment (i.e., emptying) possible by dragging me out of my present comfortable situation. It is hard for me to drag myself.

Δ

April 30, Nagoya

I returned from Easter at Lassalle's to find a large box of classical records waiting for me at school. They were from a middle-aged Japanese Catholic named John who lives in Nagoya. I met this fellow only briefly during my stay with the Trappists in Hokkaido over Christmas vacation. He also was a guest. We spoke briefly about our mutual interest in classical music.

It turns out that John has decided to enter the monastery and that his Christmas visit was the last one before entry. He has been notified of his acceptance and so is getting rid of all of his possessions. I thought his actions a bit rash so I wrote and told him that I would take care of the records for him. This response was answered by his appearance at school the other day, right in the middle of my history class. John had with him a color television, which he also pressed upon me. Now I'm holding that for him as well.

May 4, Nagoya
A Visit to Father Oshida's Community

I went up to Father Oshida's community, Takamori, the other day. I arrived on a Saturday and left the following Monday morning. Spring had just begun there and everything was approaching a green lushness that made the whole farm one rich garden of life. Oshida and I spent a lot of casual time together, culminating in a home-run baseball contest in which we tied, three to three.

In comparing Father Oshida's community with the Zen retreat house of Father Lassalle, it is obvious that both men are aware of the emptiness of a Japanese Christianity that rejects Japanese culture, yet each has responded differently. Lassalle has been studying Zen since the early 1940s and was turning Japanese Catholics to zazen more than thirty years ago. Among Catholics he is the Zen pioneer. His manner of Zen–Christian synthesis is imitative of Zen monastic culture. Father Oshida, on the other hand, is fifty-four and has been a priest for less than twenty years. He is a native Japanese and has evolved a contemplative Christianity that cleaves closely to Japanese rural life. He does not require those who come to him to become something akin to Zen monks, but instead offers them a peasant community, one in which Mass, prayers, and zazen all seem to fit. The dominant flavor of both these retreats is Japanese and contemplative.

A while ago Oshida was in Manila. There a Vietnamese nun told him of the plight of the people of her village, south of Saigon. Oshida was moved to answer her plea for assistance by arranging for a leprosy doctor to visit those afflicted in the nun's village. Two months later Oshida himself went to the village. There a priest approached him and asked Oshida to help him take care of the village orphans. He willingly agreed. Returning to Japan, Oshida soon had everyone at Takamori busily preparing clothes to be shipped to the orphans, for clothes seemed to be their initial need. His next step was to initiate an arrangement whereby some of the Vietnamese villagers could come to Takamori to experience their manner of life and, at the same time, Takamori old-timers would go to Vietnam to "train" villagers in the Takamori lifestyle. No one would stay permanently at either village; rather through cooperation he hoped to practically aid the orphans and their village in finding for themselves a Vietnamese–Christian contemplative way of life. Sadly, these plans were stymied by the Viet Cong takeover.

In conversation one evening, Oshida pointed out that in Japan nuns are far more willing to listen to his ideas than priests. The priests seem to be too caught up in the staid, conservative hierarchy. Nuns, on the other hand, feel resentful of the roles they have been obliged to assume. Too frequently they find themselves teaching kindergarten, running bookstores or whatever, their desires for Christ obscured by the work they have been told to perform. Far more of these women come to Takamori than priests.

My plans, now that school is coming to a close, are still quite nebulous. However, before I return for the second year of my teaching contract I plan to spend at least a month at Takamori, attend the late July sesshin at Lassalle's retreat house, and again visit the Trappists in Hokkaido.

... 5
Takamori in June

June 9, 1975, Takamori

I have just awakened from a nap on the farm up here in the Japan Alps. My house is a grass hut. The view is of mountain peaks. Rain outside sprinkles down on freshly planted rice. Ten yards in front of me stands a ten-foot-high wooden cross. I am at Takamori for the month of June.

All fired up to plant rice, I put on my immense, calf-high, size-thirteen rubber boots that my mother sent me from Michigan (they have returned from their Kyoto sabbatical) and headed out to the fields. When I arrived, Father Oshida took one look at my monster boots, another look at the tiny spaces between the young, fragile rice plants, and, in one solemn decree, banished me from the rice fields. So now I have a sickle in hand and I'm going out to wreak havoc on yonder small knoll of grass. With me, toddling along at three paces to my one, is a young fellow pushing three years of age. His name is Nobuhito, but he calls himself "Ba." I could tell from the first that old Ba and I were going to be good friends. Neither of us speaks much Japanese. He stands behind me as I begin to cut the grass with a neat little wrist motion. Ba is doing the same, mimicking me with an old bent stick that is half his height. He doesn't get much grass, but it sure is fun.

Evening

This afternoon I was farmed out with two others to gather hay at the dairy farm across the road. Another sickle job, this time gathering and roping. Midway through the hay gathering a rest time was declared and I, along with the twelve others who were out there, lay back on the nearest bale of hay. Closing my eyes, I heard the faint sound of music drifting over the field from a nearby elementary school. There I was, an American city boy doing farm work in the remote mountains of Japan and what was the tune? "Home on the Range."

Later we hurried to finish the work before the coming torrential rainstorm. The rain clouds appeared suddenly over the top of the mountains and we just barely got the hay in on time. Then, exhausted by the final effort, all of us sat down in a makeshift shelter out on the field and watched these dark and awesome rainclouds fill the sky.

June 12

I have not yet been told what amount of work is required of me and there is no one checking to see if I do my share. Oshida has said that Takamori is a free community, which means that everyone is free to do whatever he or she wants to do. Yesterday morning I went to take a nap after breakfast, but checked first with Oshida to see if it was all right. He said that it was all right for me to do anything that I wanted to do. One woman has spent the past few days up in her room reading and napping. No one goes to get her for work, although someone will inquire if she needs anything. I think that if I did absolutely nothing the whole time I was here, just lolled around, played ball and read, no one would say anything and few would hold a grudge.

Still, the work gets done. I'd like to think that it gets done out of an inner need in each one of us. I want to believe that the people here try to do what is best for the communal soul of the community. The more I get to know these people, the more I go through the rites of Mass and Vespers with them, the more I wonder if it is possible to have no one organizing things in a community other than the Holy Spirit. Is it possible to live a communal life without rules, without vows and still hope to come close to God? Imagine the Trappists without the Benedictine Rule to organize their lives in community, with nothing but God. The Trappists might say that the Rule is the Spirit—St. Benedict's articulation of the Spirit, a necessary scaffolding for spiritual growth. If then the Rule is one articulation of the Spirit's leadership in communal life, then can it be that living by the Spirit at Takamori is really living by an unwritten Rule? The Spirit is the Rule, and the Rule is the Spirit. Is this possible? Am I in fantasyland?

Δ

June 13

In the Bible class that followed breakfast this morning, Father Oshida made the point that in the Gospels Jesus never teaches morality; Jesus teaches only mystery. Similarly, might it be that neither the Gospels nor the Benedictine Rule organizes communities? The mystery of Jesus orders communities that seek to serve God. Without that mystery, neither morality nor community can exist.

Somewhere I remember hearing that a great deal of modern music theory stems from studies of the music of Bach. Bach's music so revolutionized earlier music forms that it set a pattern distinct from what had gone before. Modern music theories stem from what principles scholars have been able to glean from close studies of Bach's music. This broad generalization can help to explain the relationship between the Spirit and the Benedictine Rule. Bach is pure inspiration, the Spirit is pure Spirit; scholars have systematized Bach, the Rule has systematized the Spirit. You may well need the theory to understand Bach, as you may well need the Rule to live in the Spirit. Still, I want to believe that it is possible to discover both the inspiration of Bach and the movement of the Spirit without first committing to formal training in either theory or Rule.

June 17

The daily routine usually begins at five A.M. It is begun with a ringing of the community bell in Zen temple manner: long pauses after the first three rings, a crescendo, then a fourth ring. We sit and have Mass from five-thirty until seven. Breakfast is seven to eight and Bible study goes from eight until nine. All this can change at the drop of a hat, and it usually does. Generally work goes from nine until noon, then lunch and a nap until around two-thirty, followed by work until five-thirty or so. Vespers is from seven until eight, dinner eight to nine, and bed anywhere from ten minutes to three hours thereafter. The place runs on bells. Somehow things get done.

Today we have begun the first day of a quasi-sesshin. It will run three days instead of the normal seven because of the heavy summer workload. Changes in the schedule began at seven-thirty when the breakfast time and the amount of food were cut in half, then we went into a strict silence to be kept throughout the sesshin. We worked until ten, sat until noon, then had lunch, nap, work until four-thirty, a sit until six, and finally dinner and a sit from eight until nine. The sesshin takes place in a special meditation room. We sit facing the walls, one end of the room open to the summer breeze.

June 20

There is a fascinating sideshow of comings and goings here every few days. Yesterday two Little Sisters of Mercy arrived from Hong Kong. We didn't know that they were coming. No matter. Oi-san, the woman in the kitchen (and who works just about everywhere else) rolled out the tea and made them welcome. No one knows how long they will stay and no one frets about it.

People come here and find us hacking away at the grass or weeding rice, and yet I doubt that many are disappointed. There is an idyllic magic to the setting of Takamori, which, when coupled with the piety of Mass and Vespers gives the place all the structure it seems to need for providing a contemplative environment. If the people who came here just listened to some priest talk about Christ, I doubt that they would leave as satisfied as they do now. Newcomers are old hands in three days; I feel like one.

June 21

Father Oshida believes that the religious life should be led without vows. There are no vows or rules of behavior at Takamori. Still the community's contemplative needs have caused certain behaviors to develop. One of these is the practice of celibacy. Father Oshida believes that to be centrally involved at Takamori you have to be celibate. The weight of suffering, the weight of surrender necessary for the community to keep up its spiritual intensity demands that each member throw his or her full lot into the communal effort. Married couples have each other first, and that must necessarily reduce the amount of vital effort that they can offer the whole. Though no one arbitrates between celibate and married couples being members of the community, people who have married while they were members of this community have felt the need to move out of Takamori to make their own nests.

At Takamori the non-vows of poverty and obedience are also practiced. By non-vows I mean that one takes such vows implicitly as one's life grows in spiritual intensity. There is no rule saying that this community should be celibate, obedient to God, and close to the poverty line, yet these commitments have emerged as the essential ones necessary for a spiritual life here. Religious life at Takamori seems to be guided entirely by the mystery of Christ, the mystery of faith. One need not submit to vows as external impositions, however one must uncover them as internal discoveries in order to lead this life.

Takamori's life without vows has been ably assisted by its remote location and the fact that few Japanese are Christians. Most of the people who come here have chosen to be part of the less than one-percent of the Japanese population that are such. They have also chosen to travel for four or more hours to get here. Takamori is so remote that it seems that only the ardent journey here.

June 21

Ever since my arrival I have been pondering questions concerning my future. I know this questioning is futile. Still, different signals come in—some strong, some weak—and fade away. For example, I read Merton and want to become a monk—then that fades a bit. I am trying to differentiate what comes from my imagination and what comes from God. This is not easy. Like the notion of the non-vowed religious life, I am trying to discern my interior needs rather than comply with exterior rules.

Of the many conflicting signals I ponder is the call to celibacy. It has been on my mind all year. I have talked with Father Oshida about it and he has simply affirmed the possibility of this calling for me. Still, who knows?

June 23

Takamori hospitality is about to be tested to an extreme. Tomorrow at noon, Oshida and I are going to borrow the village bus, take it to Tokyo airport and pick up thirty-two visitors from India. This group gave us some forewarning (I seem to be the only person around here who frets about forewarning) and will stay for two days. The community can't handle thirty-two people in addition to the ten already here, plus whoever else happens to drop by, but again this seems to worry only me.

Δ

June 24

The tale of the visitors from India begins with a letter received by Father Oshida about two months ago from an Indian Jain priest. Jainism predates Hinduism and numbers 4.5 million followers. Jain priests are wanderers who walk barefoot from village to village. There is a Franciscan flavor to them. The letter implored Oshida to invite a party of thirty-two Indians to Takamori, including the Jain leader. Knowing little more than this, Oshida sent off an invitation. One month later he got a reply from the secretary of the World Fellowship of Religions. The letter explained that the therein listed persons, including one swami, were on a world ecumenical tour. A bit later, two weeks ago, Oshida received a brief letter stating their arrival time at the Tokyo airport. Unaware of their plans, yet worried about the travel time and expense from Takamori to Tokyo, Oshida had me call India and ask the Fellowship secretary if he knew that they were coming to a primitive farm off in the mountains and not to a great Japanese temple. The secretary said that he understood, so off we went, Oshida and I, to pick them up at the airport. That was June 21.

We drove to the airport in a bus that had been donated by the nearby town of Fujimi in the hope that the visit of the Indians would spur the meager tourist industry of the town. While we were driving to the airport, everyone at Takamori was in a flurry preparing enough sleeping space for the Indians.

We got to the airport forty-five minutes early. As we waited in the reception room we were joined by all kinds of Zen, Shingon, name-your-sect Buddhists, and others. Everyone was formally dressed, except for Oshida in his baggy pants and me in my sneakers. While the Indians were going through customs, a friend of Oshida's who spoke Hindi arrived. This fellow thought it odd that such a large delegation of Indians would have little-known Takamori as its host. With the arrival hall now jam-packed with what looked like an ad-hoc ecumenical conference, we began to wonder too. Just then we ran across a rather official-looking man, flanked by two assistants, and carrying a two-page printed itinerary of the World Fellowship of Religions visit to Tokyo. We were nowhere on the schedule.

It turned out that the Rissho-kai, a new Buddhist sect in Japan, was expecting to sponsor the Indians. The Rissho-kai had been communicating with the Indians, as had we, but apparently the Indians thought that Takamori and the Rissho-kai were one and the same, and we each received half the correspondence. The upshot of this debacle was that we would interject ourselves into the Rissho-kai schedule for a day and a half of the four days we now learned the Indians were planning to stay in Japan.

The Indians entered the room. Only seventeen, and thirteen of these businessmen. The other four included a frail orange-robed swami, and three small, white-robed, mouths-covered-with-white-cards, white mops-slung-over-their-shoulders, Jain priests. One was Mujini, the head of the religion.

Piling them all into our bus, now bound for the Rissho-kai headquarters for the day then to Takamori for the night, I got a chance to ask some of the businessmen just what they were up to. They told me that in 2,500 years no Jain priest had ever ridden in a cart or a car and much less an airplane. Mujini had now taken this unprecedented step in order to whip up an ecumenical drive in India and throughout the world. So precedent-shattering were his actions that fifteen followers (the rest of the thirty-two) had decided not to come along. He and his troupe were seen off by thousands of people in New Delhi. The swami was Swami Chidananda, head of a large ashram in India and one of the moving forces in a movement that has spawned a number of Yoga ashrams in the United States. He eats little more than warm milk, they told me. The businessmen themselves were providing capital for this venture and came along as an entourage.

So there we were, Oshida and I, in our farmer's clothes in a borrowed bus hauling members of the World Fellowship of Religions around Tokyo. Irony verged on farce when we got to the well appointed Rissho-kai headquarters. In the next several hours the two of us hoboed through a very formal reception, with some in tuxedos, and a seven-course dinner in a plush dining room. At dinner several of the businessmen watched to see if the Mujini saw them drinking liquor, taboo in Jainism.

At eight in the evening we left the Rissho-kai and headed for the mountains. Mujini did get a chance to speak with the head of the Rissho-kai, everyone was happy about the possibility of setting up yet another institution for the study of world-wide ecumenicism, and Oshida and I started to get this sinking feeling that the high-flying businessmen would find it difficult to adapt to Takamori.

Everything, as usual, turned out all right. The kitchen fed the businessmen and Oshida talked with the Mujini. I got a chance to spend some time with Swami Chidananda, so let me say something about that.

I was given the job of taking Swami Chidananda to his room. When we got to the room, Chidananda asked if that was a pump organ over in the corner. Indeed it was, and before I could respond he had gone over and

sat down. Bracing myself for some unearthly Hindu music, I was not prepared to hear one of the bounciest renditions of "Old Black Joe" I've heard
in some time. From this opener Swami Chidananda swung into "Camp-
town Races" and we were stomping and doo-dahing around the room for
the next several minutes. Soon we were just hanging out together, talking
about the latest blister on the swami's right toe and the crack in the ceiling.
The great Swami Chidananda was also a nice guy.

Because of the highly ritualized state of the Jain religion, Mujini was
more difficult to get to know. Up until the day before he came to Japan, I
was told, he had never eaten food on a table or in the presence of priests
outside Jainism. His two disciples guarded him closely. However in the
evening of his stay, the Mujini gave a talk on his practices. My notes from
that talk follow.

The fundamental belief of the Jains is nonviolence. The Mujini says
that he has no personal rights, yet it is his responsibility to respect the personal rights of others. He practices nonviolence through a purity of food
(no meat, eggs, or onions) and a purity of body. The pure body belief has
evolved a number of distinctive traits. The white card held over the mouth
by string around the ears is intended to keep him from swallowing insects.
The small white mop slung over the shoulder is used to clear dust and
insects from a place where he is about to sit. He wears white robes and follows a vow of celibacy.

The practice of nonviolence also involves surrender to the ultimate
powers of the universe. This devotion to the ultimate is intended to eventually bring about unity with God and true wisdom. Devotion is practically
achieved through ten different yoga postures and two different breathing
practices applied according to personal type. The beginner eventually
becomes sufficiently skilled in his particular posture to move on to a study
of the three currents of energy that travel from the lower spinal column to
the head, and the ten rivulets of energy that deposit into these three
columns. The disciple is supposed to concentrate upon the rivulets one at a
time after receiving instructions from his master on how to find them.

Next is a study of the seven psychic centers or chakras that extend from
the lower spinal column to the top of the head, with stations at the solar
plexus and between the eyebrows, to name two. To activate these centers
two mantra words have evolved; OM activates the nerves around the navel
and ARHUM activates the area around the bottom of the spinal column.

Next comes meditation on the psychic centers through a one-pointed
concentration on the third eye. This is accomplished by putting a finger
on the tip of the nose and watching it as it rises to the space between the

eyebrows. Of course you can't see up there, but Mujini says that if you try to do it you will notice that your gaze "locks in" and the third eye area suddenly comes alive. Another way to do this he says, is to focus your eyes, or inner eye, on that spot. In zazen, I believe it is like looking at a spot on the floor or just gazing at nothing. These are the basics. Now the beginner begins.

Mujini, Swami Chidananda, and party left on a bus for Tokyo after staying at Takamori for a day and two nights. The question they left hanging was why they were touring the world giving speeches on ecumenicism. What this group apparently wants to do is build a huge ecumenical center in New Delhi with a church for every faith—a sort of religious United Nations.

June 25

Sesshin at Takamori are flexible affairs. According to the needs of the community, Father Oshida can adjust the length of sittings, hours of sleep, amount and nature of the work, type and quantity of food, length of community silences, and so forth. For example he has just announced an interesting hybrid, you might call it the "eternal sesshin." Nobody knows when it will end. Actually, it is the "indefinite quasi-sesshin," because there is less sitting than a regular sesshin. I guess the word *sesshin* now begins to lose its meaning. I will just say that things are getting more intense and leave it at that.

Sesshin here serve the purpose of keeping the place in a contemplative mood. The current sesshin has probably been called because we have a number of new people in the community whom I think are going to have to either buckle down or leave. But nobody is going to kick them out. The sesshin will do it. They don't even have to go to the sittings. But then they will feel out of harmony with the community. Rather than put up signs and threaten people to fall in line, Oshida just calls a sesshin and things fall in place.

June 26

I remember Father Aquinas at Spencer once telling me that he was never bored at the monastery. After a short time here at Takamori, I think I can see what he meant. Though things are usually intense, people and events have a way of phasing in and out that makes it difficult to be bored.

Abruptly today the sesshin ends. We have to prepare for a wedding. Still the sesshin had the needed effect. The five hours of sitting were coupled with five hours of rigorous work in the fields. In the course of this daily scheme, there were several sudden illnesses and some people who had planned to stay longer left. I found the five hours of work in the rice fields, bent over in a touch toe position, to be especially tough (it was my first work in the fields since Father Oshida decided that the plants were now strong enough to survive my large boot tracks). Though there is no limit to how much or how little we are to work, I decided to commit myself to five hours every day. But only five hours. I was checking my watch every fifteen minutes.

June 27

There are two North American sisters here today. Each has received special permission to live outside of her respective mission in Tokyo in order to be near Yamada Roshi. Yamada Roshi runs a layperson's zendo in Kamakura, south of Tokyo. The zendo is something like a local church for the people of the area. There is a sit in the morning and one in the evening plus bimonthly sesshin. One of the sisters told me that her day began with the office of Matins at home, then a sit at the zendo, followed by Lauds and Mass at the home of a German Benedictine abbot who lives nearby (a separate story that I would like to pursue). In the evening she does two more hours of sitting at the zendo.

June 28

Though I am frequently enthusiastic about the benefits of Zen for Christian spiritual development, I still have doubts. This afternoon I had a wide-ranging conversation with Father Oshida about "Zennie" Christians. These are Christians whom Oshida feels have gone too far into Zen, so that there is a sterile feel to them. They are highly disciplined and no doubt well along on their paths, yet this closed focus on Zen—while not denying Christianity—makes them seem less joyful. There is not a feeling of awed wonder and opening out to the world. Zen seems so much more closed, black and white, austere. I think Brother Aidan hit it on the head when he asked about grace in Buddhism. There does not appear to be a doctrine of grace in Buddhism. Being too "Zennie" is being too reliant upon a prodigious self-effort, a honing in on one's practice rather than an opening out through one's practice.

June 30

There is a young man here who is going through his private struggle so graphically that it takes little insight to understand his trial. He came unannounced from Hong Kong, deposited here by his mother in the hope that farm life would shape up his rowdy bachelor's life. He does not want to be here, though he says he does. He endures, but his good intentions are beginning to weaken. He cannot sit in Zen meditation posture for more than a few minutes, he avoids manual work, and no one speaks his language. Eventually he will probably leave, but he must decide this on his own. Now he endures. Two days ago he got angry and walked out of the rice field work. Yesterday he went into town and bought some rock music tapes and a tape recorder. We all endured through an evening of raucous music. No telling what he is going to do today. He is playing out in caricature some of the inner struggles I imagine we all face here. Though his actions irritate me, in many ways I am like him.

July 1

There were once chairs and a high altar in the community chapel. Then one day, after the chairs and altar had been temporarily taken down to make room for some people who needed a place to sleep, Oshida realized that it was more natural to have Mass on the floor in the zazen posture. Done.

Once a Buddhist monk was present for Mass. After sitting for a while he rose, just before the Mass was to begin, and silently went about rapping each person present with his *kyosaku* (the stick used in Zen monasteries by the jikijitsu to awaken meditators). After completing his ritual the monk solemnly presented the stick to Oshida for future use, and the Mass began.

July 2

If I wanted to become a priest, but not a monk, could I go through seminary in a contemplative environment? Does such a seminary exist? Why do priestly training and contemplation appear so antithetical? What about a contemplative seminary that does not ask for monastic vows?

Δ

July 3

Today I have been singing one of the work songs that has emerged from the field work at Takamori. Father Oshida believes that sacred songs should take root in work songs. The most sacred songs sung on this farm are those composed while working in the fields.

Perhaps it is just that I am the city boy having his first full fling at farming life. Still I feel a wonderful exhaustion here at the end of the day that is more valuable to me than any intellectual or anxiety-spawned exhaustion I have felt at the end of a school day. It is an exhaustion that reaches down into the marrow of my bones, that makes me walk more slowly because I am too tired to walk any faster. It makes me glad for the evening meal, glad for the chatter of my friends, for the simple joys of life. No amount of pondering upon life's verities can grant me this wonderful exhaustion. I must go out there and work all day for it to be given to me.

In a few days I will return to Nagoya for a few weeks, then in late July I plan to head to Tokyo for a sesshin at Father Lassalle's Zen retreat house.

6
Sesshin

Schedule for the July Sesshin

4:00–4:20 A.M.	Rise
4:20–5:00	Zazen
5:00–6:00	Mass
6:00–7:00	Breakfast and work
7:30–8:10	Zazen
8:10–8:30	Kinhin and interval
8:30–9:40	Lecture and interval
9:40–10:20	Zazen (Dokusan)
10:20–10:30	Interval
10:30–11:00	Zazen
11:00–11:30	Lunch
1:30–2:10	Zazen
2:10–2:30	Kinhin
2:30–3:10	Zazen (Dokusan)
3:10–3:20	Interval
3:20–3:50	Zazen
3:50–4:30	Optional zazen
4:30–5:00	Supper
6:20–7:00	Zazen
7:00–7:20	Kinhin and interval
7:20–8:00	Zazen
8:00–8:20	Kinhin and interval
8:20–9:00	Zazen (Tea)
9:00	Retire

I
am at Father Lassalle's Zen retreat house awaiting the arrival of twenty-five sesshin fans. We will have an even number of men and women and nearly half will be members of religious orders. The sesshin will last seven days with more than eight hours of meditation each day. I will be burrowing into the slow repetition of "Lord Have Mercy," if my legs do not give out. I feel like I'm about to run the marathon and must pace myself. I have to somehow keep focused upon my prayer and not allow the sitting to deteriorate into a leg pain endurance contest.

First Day

This afternoon I've been getting a good look at zazen as athletic encounter. Toward the end of the last two rounds of the afternoon sittings, I gave up all pretense of meditation and just tried to hold my posture until the bell. Success at this endurance game brings a feeling of relief and accomplishment that is similar to the feeling I used to have after breaking personal records in track and field. These are pleasant moments for sure, but I question whether they are beneficial for spiritual growth. Perhaps enduring is a marginal benefit, the goal of one sort of body discipline.

Evening

Soto and Rinzai are the two major schools in Japanese Buddhism. Rinzai places emphasis on attaining a definite spiritual state, *satori* or enlightenment. This state must be certified by a Rinzai roshi who has in turn had his enlightenment certified by his roshi. Soto, on the other hand, considers enlightenment to be a more relative state than the Rinzai people might allow. Rather than emphasize reaching the "goal" of enlightenment, Soto masters place greater importance upon the gradual ripening of their students through long hours of meditation.

A further difference between Rinzai and Soto is the former's use of koans, special formula questions like "What is the sound of one hand clapping?"—which can only be answered through a change in consciousness. Soto, on the other hand, uses what might be called the "natural" koan of one's existence. This is not a koan at all. Rather it is the fundamental unspoken question of "Why am I here?" or "Who am I?" that nags at the heart of every thoughtful human being. Rinzai koans are attempts to articulate this dilemma through a series of irrational questions. The Soto "natural" koan *is* this unspoken yet universal question.

The spiritual growth encouraged by Soto masters, I imagine, is similar to the ever-deepening union with God experienced by Christian contemplatives. Neither Soto nor Christianity lays emphasis upon reaching an endpoint, enlightenment. Furthermore Soto's "natural" koan can be likened to the void, the emptiness in each Christian that propels him or her toward God. Additionally neither the Soto Zen master nor the Christian spiritual director has to be enlightened to be a spiritual guide. In contrast, Rinzai emphasizes the pursuit of a definite goal, through the use of a specific method that, if successful, should grant the student an objective credential. Despite Soto's more apparent similarities to Christianity, most meditating Christians I know are more attracted to the Rinzai approach.

Perhaps this is because there are no overt, built-in standards in either Soto or Christianity that assure the seeker that the roshi or the spiritual director is speaking from experience when he or she tries to guide the student toward a deeper awareness. Christians who feel that the spiritual rigor and mystical depth has been lost in the Christianity of modern times are attracted to Rinzai's more clear-cut, standardized system of spiritual growth. They feel that modern Christians have become too easily satisfied with a God perceived solely through conceptual thinking. I know that this is why I have been attracted to Rinzai. At the same time, those of us Christians who are interested in Zen must try to keep ourselves from pursuing enlightenment as a goal, but, rather, see it as a grace from God that may or may not come at some point along the unending way.

Second Day

A little over a year ago, I discussed the meaning of Catholic dogma with Father Raphael at Spencer. Father Raphael said that dogma was essentially mystery. This suggested to me that dogma might best be characterized as a subjective conceptualization of an objective reality that transcends words, concepts, and images. In that way I began to understand certain points of dogma, especially the Trinity, as similar to Zen koans. These doctrines could never be understood literally, but only through meditation on their mystery could one come to some glimmer of their inner meaning. As I see it, the words of Christian dogma and the words of Zen koans cannot be fully understood literally, instead each has as its purpose the sharpening of our focus on a transcendent reality.

I have always found it difficult to think through Catholic dogma, and especially the Trinity. Words and thoughts that lead me to the latter always seem to get me lost in other, more distracting, thoughts. I have found it easier to deal with the Trinity if I realize first its similarity to a koan. The Trinity is like a koan of the Rinzai school. It is a special formula that has lying behind it the natural koan of our existence. Similarly, Catholic dogma is the gateway of an ever-deepening mystery that cannot be put into words. To better understand Catholic dogma I might meditate upon it as Rinzai students meditate upon their koans.

Third Day

We're well into the third day of the sesshin and everybody's legs are sore. This afternoon we had ten minutes between sittings and all of us went out into the hall and proceeded to look like a track team loosening up for a meet. There is a wonderful old German priest sitting near me. Occasionally he offers a few words of encouragement in his heavy German accent. After a particularly tough sitting this afternoon, I saw him coming out of the bathroom with his pants rolled up to his knees and water dripping from his legs. He apparently had his own home remedy for leg pain. With a broad, child's smile on his face, he said to me with a laugh "Just da ting!" So I went in and rolled up my pants and did it too. He was right, "Just da ting!"

Fourth Day

Today on the fourth day of the sesshin, in the twenty-eighth hour of sitting, I've decided that my legs cannot take it any longer. I was enduring along yesterday when I went to speak to Father Lassalle during dokusan. I told him that most of the time that I spent in the zendo was wasted just enduring the pain from my legs. I was spending little time with my prayer. Father Lassalle asked if there was another posture that I might find easier. I suggested the Burmese (legs parallel, not folded) and he said to give it a try. Well this morning I tried but it was the same old story. I don't see how I can break through the pain barrier. My problem is that I don't know to what degree my physical pain is an illusion. To push pain is to be either a fool or a saint, I figure, depending upon the circumstances.

Δ

Afternoon

I spoke with Father Lassalle again and he recommended merging with the pain, making the pain my koan.

Fifth Day

Yesterday at this time I had already packed my bags and checked the bus schedule. But after talking again with Lassalle I decided to stay for another hour or two. I'm still here and probably I will finish the sesshin. For reasons unknown to me, my legs do not hurt as much, or perhaps I've gotten used to the pain. So things are on an upbeat. I'm no longer simply enduring the pain but I am again focusing upon the "Lord Have Mercy."

Afternoon

Since Father Lassalle is not yet a roshi (though I hear he is close), I think it is appropriate to think of him as a meditation instructor. In the Buddhist context, he is something like some of the teachers in the Soto tradition. These guides are able to direct you along the path of meditation but unable to confirm enlightenment.

In Christianity acts of faith are directed toward God. In practical terms this might mean that when a Catholic is given the choice of meditating in the presence of the Blessed Sacrament or not in its presence, he or she will elect the former. The presence of the Blessed Sacrament would probably not affect a Buddhist in a similar situation. The Christian reliance upon a savior is countered with the Buddhist emphasis on self-effort. The one is religious in the sense that a religion must be dualistic, the other is existential. Buddhism has indeed been called atheistic for just this lack of dualism.

Now why is it that the religious West today is drawn to the East? In terms of Christianity and Zen, I think it is due to the lack of emphasis upon the existential, self-effort aspects of Christianity. I think that for too long there has been a misunderstanding of what reliance upon God really means. Christianity is not all reliance upon God, if we understand such a reliance to mean a sort of sitting down on the curb and giving up because God is running the show. Christian reliance upon God means total self-effort and yet total self-surrender. Christian self-effort is all wrapped up in the terms "waiting" and "watching." The idea that "time is made for waiting" strikes right at the heart of the matter. How do we wait? How do we rely on God? What do we do while sitting on the curb and letting God run the show? Taking a tip from the Zen folks we might sit in zazen, for isn't zazen, that total self-effort, what is truly meant by waiting for God? Buddhists in their zazen and Christians in their many forms of waiting are both told not to expect anything. The fundamental difference is that the Buddhists expect a pay-off, but to Christians it shouldn't really matter.

Evening

Tonight seems to be the night for kneecap pain. I got hit with it along with the rest and now we're all out in the hall doing kneecap exercises. The leg pain is not so bad, but it still has its moments. A few rounds ago I peeked a look at my watch and was astonished to discover that there were still twenty minutes of sitting left in that round. I doubted that I could make it so I began to scramble, think up diversions like counting the seconds or slowly swaying my body back and forth. However, midway through the scrambling, I thought of a better way. If I can be with Christ on his cross at these moments, as Father Thomas suggested in a recent letter (March 8) then my pain can be his and I can suffer with him in his passion.

Sixth Day

I began this sesshin sitting in a quarter-lotus, switched to a half, then because of the pain went back to the quarter. Today for the first time I did a sustained half-lotus with one cushion rather than two. I also lowered my gaze to a one-yard distance on the floor in front of me. As a result I felt a distinct shift in gears. The leg pain was there but my consciousness was somehow deeper than the pain so I only felt it when I went up from the deeper place. I felt below all emotions, like a rock. Furthermore there was little sense of self, it was as though I had merged with the energy of the room. I was deeper for a longer time than I have been so far this sesshin. This is the most extraordinary experience I have had in meditation. I'm going to try to forget about it and get back to the daily rounds.

Afternoon

I spoke with Father Lassalle. He told me that the above described experience is called *zanmai*, apparently one of the many markers along the path to enlightenment. I will try to forget about this immediately.

Seventh Day

Sesshin's last day. The scripture line "Heaven and Earth shall pass away but my Lord will not pass away" keeps going through my mind.

These seven days I have learned that there is a transcendent place cutting deep below all pain and normal experience. Oshida's farm advocates the living of the fruits of Christian contemplation—and suggests cultivating the roots of these fruits through hard work and zazen. Lassalle too seeks to live these fruits, but he tends to put a greater emphasis on pushing you so that you may someday arrive at the true depths of Christian spirituality. Perhaps intensive meditation, much more than the ample amount at Oshida's, is needed to come to this greater depth. So my question is this: Is the intensive meditation of monastic Zen an avenue to deeper Christian spirituality, or is it more surely a path to an unnecessary asceticism?

7

On the Road

Since leaving the sesshin at Father Lassalle's retreat house, I have hitch-hiked north to a coastal town several hundred miles north of Tokyo. Here I will spend the night at a youth hostel before continuing north to Hokkaido, where I hope to spend a week on retreat with the Trappist monks near Hakodate. This evening I've been walking along the beach and thinking, I don't know why, about the historical Jesus.

Sasaki Roshi once asked the monks at the Spencer monastery what would happen if it were discovered that Jesus never lived. I believe that would be the end of Christianity, for our religion is built upon our dependence upon Jesus to lead us to the Father. We cannot reach God on our own. On the other hand, if it were discovered that the Buddha never lived it would probably not matter a great deal to Buddhists. This is because Buddhists must ultimately rely on their own efforts and not, as in Christianity, upon the intercession of a savior. The contrast between these two responses stresses the importance of the existence of Jesus for Christians.

Still, would not Christianity be more palatable if emphasis was placed only upon the transcendent, risen Christ? Buddhists who are sympathetic to Christianity appreciate the words of the revealed Christ, especially as they are written in the Gospel of John. And the Japanese people to whom the Christian missionaries preach, I am told, are more drawn to Scripture as eternal truth that comes through and transcends the Gospel narratives than they are attracted to the particulars of Jesus' life. Furthermore, eminent people like the historian Arnold Toynbee have said that in order for Christianity to be a universal religion it must drop its insistence upon the historicity of Jesus. So why do Christians so strongly stress the importance of the life of Jesus? Because without his historical life among us we could never come to know the grace of God. Without the incarnation of Jesus, we would be thrown back upon only our self-efforts. God has become man in Jesus: this is our faith. Without the incarnation, Christianity could not exist.

July 31, Lake Towada

I'm in a youth hostel on the southern rim of Lake Towada in a mountainous section of northern Japan. Today I've covered three-hundred miles, hitched rides with seven or eight different cars, and talked my pidgin Japanese to everyone I met. I will stay here for a day or two and then continue north. This is an area not used to foreigners, so it is pretty difficult for me to just fade into the scenery.

Throughout my day I have been troubled by my experiences back at the sesshin. I'm referring to that alleged zanmai experience, or deep recollection, that occurred to me on the sesshin's fourth day. What baffles me most is my inability to place that moment on any previous chart of my experience. And yet the rhetoric that follows gives the right verbal sense. To be beyond pain, beyond joy or sorrow, to be more like a rock or a tree than a human being is—frankly, frightening!

August 1, Lake Towada

Father Oshida once had a discussion with a Zen master in which he asked if the roshi's enlightenment was the same as that of the Buddha's. The master responded that it was, it had to be. Oshida said that the roshi was wrong. Astonished, the master asked why. "The effect is different" was Oshida's response.

Father Oshida told me this story to illustrate his belief that the Zen enlightenment is of no value if there is not a consonant change in compassion. Theoretically every enlightenment should be the same as that of the Buddha and so be filled with compassion. The enlightened person is an open, loving person in whose presence you feel at home. Furthermore, Oshida says, enlightenment is not an endpoint and not a goal to be sought. There is no "making it"—just a continual further absorption into God. However, over the many years since the Buddha's great moment, a more relative understanding of enlightenment has evolved. So now it is apparently possible for someone to attain enlightenment and yet remain a selfish, abrasive sort.

This is not solely a problem of Zen Buddhism. In the latter part of Father Lassalle's book, *Zen Meditation for Christians*,[1] he refers to John Ruysbroeck's conclusion concerning errant Christians who had genuine mystical experiences but were lacking in Christian love of neighbor. Ruysbroeck acknowledges the experience of these people as genuine and in no way does he attempt to degrade their mystical moments; however, he does criticize their total self-concern and warns against emulating them. Ruysbroeck's dispute with his selfish mystics is similar to Oshida's criticism of the Zen master. Both appear to suffer from an excessive focus upon themselves.

August 2, Hakodate

Yesterday I covered about a sixth of Japan. After hitching all morning I took a three-hour ferry ride to the northern island of Hokkaido. I arrived at the port of Hakodate around dinner time. There are both Trappists and Trappistines on the outskirts of this city and even an Eastern Orthodox church, but in the midst of the city, yesterday anyway, the gala annual Shinto festival was held. Soon after enjoying the festival, I discovered that there wasn't any space in the local youth hostel. So I wound up going out to the Trappists late at night and sleeping on the grounds until morning. It then turned out that there was no room for me at their guesthouse for tonight or any other night this week. I should have made a reservation. Still, I did get to spend the day at the monastery.

In the afternoon Abbot Bonaventure gave me a ride back into town. We stopped along the way and had chocolate parfaits high atop Hakodate's largest department store.

I'm going to take the ferry over to the main island today, and then start a leisurely hitch back down to Takamori tomorrow. There I will spend a few days before returning to Nagoya to begin preparations for the coming school year.

August 15, Takamori

Several years ago when I stayed for two weeks at a Sasaki Roshi's Rinzai Zen center in southern California, I met a young man who had been

---

1. H. M. Enomiya Lassalle, *Zen Meditation for Christians* (LaSalle, Ill.: Open Court, 1974), 101.

there for over a year. He seemed to be under a great deal of pressure and, in speaking with me, said that he felt like a capped soda bottle unable to explode. His motives for coming to Mt. Baldy did not seem to be well-reasoned, still he had managed to stay there through several sesshins and a year of manual work. What had apparently guided him through the year was the conviction that he would stay there at all costs. The cost seemed to have been his psychological stability, for rather than improve from his stay at the Zen center he seemed to have gotten worse. To be with him was to be immediately aware of the strain he was undergoing.

This fellow was admitted to Mt. Baldy along with everyone else. It was believed that the spiritual environment would heal him. But the roots seemed to have been planted wrong. He was not properly motivated, and yet he stubbornly hung on, substituting brute self-will for broader reflection and, as a result, seemed only to be getting worse. The problem of wrongly motivated, strong-willed people is one that probably plagues all open, intensely spiritual communities. This problem is also present at Takamori.

I returned here a week ago to learn that one of the young men was now under observation at a sanatorium. From what I have gathered, he was one such strong-willed person who had been throwing all his energy into a blind self-discipline (very Japanese). When I knew him he certainly seemed tight, serious, and strained, but I didn't think his case was that serious. I was wrong.

Do people like this fellow or the one at Mt. Baldy benefit from staying at these communities or should they be somehow screened out? The normal self-screening procedure of "spiritual intensity" did not work in either of these cases. Perhaps they should have been coaxed out at an earlier time? The Trappists have now adopted such procedures, should the same be done at Takamori? But Oshida stakes so much on "free to come—free to go" in this community that to screen would be to impose human designs on God's providence.

August 23, Nagoya

I went to Lassalle's for a sesshin and lasted one day. I was physically tired and psychologically unprepared. You just can not breeze through a sesshin.

September 12, Takamori

I am at Oshida's for the weekend. I made the last day of a sesshin and have just spent the evening with one of the participants, a Trappist. His name is Father Luke, he is forty-six years old and his home monastery is in Europe.

Father Luke entered his monastery at the age of twenty, remained there for twenty years, then was ordered by his abbot to be the priest-in-residence at one of the Trappistine monasteries in the south of Japan. He arrived six years ago and soon became aware of Zen. He started sitting on his own, was later introduced to a Rinzai roshi, and last year he wrote his superior informing him of his intention to enter, on a trial basis, a Rinzai monastery. Luke's superior disapproved of these plans, but things were somehow left undecided. He went to the monastery and stayed for one year, leaving only fifteen days ago.

Father Luke has not renounced Christianity. He tells me, however, that the strict discipline and absolute lack of privacy in the Zen temple kept him from saying Mass each day. He does not believe it possible to do zazen back at his home monastery without a roshi. He wants to be in a Christian community, he also wants to do zazen, and he cannot buy my argument that a truly developed Christian spiritual director can fill his need for a roshi.

Father Luke is waiting here at Takamori for further word from his superior. He fears orders to return to Europe.

October 19, Kyoto

I have just completed two days of a sesshin at Kyoto's Antai-ji Soto Zen Temple. The temple is the congregating point for a great number of Japan's foreign seekers, most of whom are American. Antai-ji has been transformed to be of service to these men and women who have shown enough determination to come here on their own. The foreigners range in age from twenty-five to thirty-five. Ten have been in Japan for more than four years, three are monks. The Japanese monks number more than a dozen. There has not been a roshi here since the recent retirement of Uchiyama Roshi (author of *Approach to Zen*). There is a head priest though and there is zazen: twelve hours of sitting in one sesshin day; one five-day and one three-day sesshin a month. This is a lot of zazen. But Antai-ji is a Soto temple and Soto's emphasis is on sitting.

At Antai-ji I feel I have arrived at a place in the long wake of the pioneering generation of foreigners that came here before me. I am a second, or even third, generation foreign seeker here in Japan. The road was much more difficult for those who came in the 1950s and even earlier. Then few Japanese knew English and I am told that most Zen people were fairly hostile toward seekers from the West. Now I experience some language difficulties, but always there has been some enterprising American who has talked to such and such a monk before, and so the way is somewhat prepared for each of my encounters. The culture shock was probably much greater for those who came before me. Though I do not know who most of these people were (outside of the poet Gary Snyder and the Zen master Philip Kapleau), I owe them a great deal. Once in a while I meet one of them, an older American monk at a Zen monastery.

I like Antai-ji; there is none of the bothersome ritual here that I had gotten to dislike at Sasaki Roshi's Zen center in California and at Father Lassalle's Zen retreat house. Though absolute silence is observed and there are but three twenty-minute periods of free time each sesshin day, the discipline seems to come more from within each student rather than being imposed by an authoritarian leader. The Americans whom I have met have gone out of their way to help me fit in. The Japanese monks have been just as thoughtful; together everyone has worked to minimize friction and focus attention on the meditation.

One downside, though, is the lack of an overt moral code for those who are neither Christian nor Buddhist. This is not to say that there is a lot of debauchery at Antai-ji, just that there is neither dogma nor leader to say "no." Many Zen adherents, especially foreigners, are not necessarily Buddhists. Their primary interest is the technique of zazen and the discipline of sesshin. They are devotees of sitting and not moral doctrines. My gut feeling is that morality is ultimately a question of energy—how to conserve it and how not to blow it away in a useless manner. Doing meditation you conserve energy; engaging in casual sex or going out and getting drunk, feeling jealous, or wallowing in self-pity, you blow that energy away. A religion's moral code helps you through these problems; if you don't have a religion, then shouldn't you at least have your own moral rules?

Five years ago an American lady came to Antai-ji from Northampton, Massachusetts. She was interested in Zen and, after returning home, sent money to Uchiyama Roshi to enable him to send a monk to start a Zen center in Northampton. I knew something of this when I was a student at Amherst College, near Northampton, because it was rumored that the driver of the college bus was involved in Zen (which he was, two of his friends were sitting with me at Antai-ji). A small Zen center did get started in Northampton and now in the last six months Antai-ji has sent another Japanese monk and a couple of the more experienced Americans to a six-acre plot of land fifteen miles north of Northampton. There they have joined some of the Northampton Zen people and have begun working a small farm and building a zendo.

November 1, Nagoya

I've just returned from a weekend in Kamakura, one of the more ancient and revered cities in Japan. Many foreigners go there to study with the maverick Yamada Roshi. This Zen master is married, runs his zendo out of his house in a fashionable neighborhood, and teaches his own hybrid of Soto and Rinzai techniques. He also tries to accommodate foreigners, a number of whom are older women who seem to have come here after years of marriage and raising a family. Yamada has granted roshi status to one of them. He also has an American student who is now a roshi in Hawaii. In addition, the two Catholic sisters I met at Oshida's are studying here, and one of them is said to be well along in her practice.

When I arrived in Kamakura, I first went to the residence of Father Odo Haas, a German Benedictine abbot who was for many years the abbot of a monastery in South Korea. Two years ago he came to Japan to begin a Bene-dictine foundation and settled in Kamakura. Father Haas knows Yamada Roshi and through conversations with him he has become interested in Zen. More than anything else, I found Father Haas to be a solid, caring person—one, like Father Thomas, in whom I could confide. He gave me some good guidance on some specifically Catholic matters that had been on my mind.

Father Haas does some sitting and there are others who live with him who are regular students of Yamada Roshi. One of these is my European Trappist friend Father Luke. The last time I saw Luke was at Father Oshida's farm where he was waiting for word from his superior on whether or not he could stay in Japan to study Zen. Now he is planning to stay with Father Haas and study with Yamada Roshi.

Δ

November 4, Nagoya

Today I have been reading John Dalrymple's little book *Theology and Spirituality*, sent to me by Father Thomas. Here for the first time I have run across the distinction between positive and negative theology. As I understand it, positive theology is that corpus of knowledge that we have about God and his revelation in human terms. It is written dogma, scripture, intellectual ideas, spoken prayer. Negative theology emphasizes the infinite gap between our concepts of God and the reality of God. It does not deny positive theology so much as it augments it by pointing out that God is really so much more than any concept or symbol or prayer we might use to try to envelop him. Dalrymple argues that the negative approach has to grow out of the positive approach.

> Unknowing must be preceded by knowing, prayer by Bible reading and contemporary thought. . . . The two approaches need each other. Nobody is entitled to choose only one form of knowledge; he must choose both, correcting the self-confidence of positive theology with the pessimism of negative theology. If there is too much unknowing of God, our knowledge of him will get thinner and thinner as time goes on for lack of sustenance from the Bible, not to mention cross-fertilization from the culture of the day, and spirituality will become a dusty abstraction out of touch with living thought.[2]

My hunch is that Christianity and zazen should work together much like positive and negative theology. They are like a two-stage rocket. Zen meditation is not the same as silent prayer, the infused contemplation of Christianity, if it is not driven to its heights by Christian positive theology. Christians who deny this and place extra emphasis on their zazen at the expense of scripture study and discursive prayer are perhaps not well-grounded in an openended positive theology or are in rebellion against a too thorough indoctrination in a narrowminded positive theology. I imagine that it is possible for people in either instance to lose their Christian roots.

Δ

---

2. John Dalrymple, *Theology and Spirituality* (Notre Dame, Ind.: Fides Publishers, 1970), 18.

A Letter from Brother Simon

November 16, Spencer

With Christmas just around the corner, I thought I would drop you a note to wish you a most blessed Christmas. This is a feast very dear to the Cistercians, and to all Christians. Sometimes weak souls are filled with awe and a certain amount of fear in contemplating the Passion and Death of Christ, but Christmas reassures them and fills them with light and joy.

Your letters are really enjoyable and make us share in some way your search for God. I guess that is what life is all about, and it is the chief thing St. Benedict would have us find in a novice: "That he truly seek God."

Δ

A Letter from Father Thomas

November 17, Spencer

Your letters have been coming in very faithfully. We enjoy them very much; in fact, I share them with Father Bernard McVeigh, the abbot of Guadalupe who is very interested in Zen.

I wish you could get more exposure to Christian, and specifically Catholic, theology and spirituality. I'm glad that you found in Father Haas a good priest in whom you can confide.

... *8*
Leaving Japan

I have decided to leave Japan at the beginning of this coming summer. I think I have gathered most of the information I came seeking. This does not mean that I know all that there is to know about Zen and Christianity, but that I think I have found enough answers to my questions so that staying on in Japan is no longer imperative. A further commitment here would mean a prolonged stay at Father Oshida's community, and though I am attracted to Takamori, I would like to make this more serious commitment in the United States. A Christian contemplative life that uses zazen as a spiritual practice cannot be too foreign in an America now subject to overtures from so many diverse faiths.

December 28, 1975, Nagoya

For me to stay in Japan would mean a commitment to a Western Christianity that is trying to adapt to Japanese roots. I am not Japanese. I am an American. This is something which I have heretofore laughed off but which is becoming a more viable reason for returning home the longer I stay here. I am most interested in a universal, contemplative Christianity sown in American soil, a Christianity enlightened by the East, buttressed by the insights that can surely be found here and still just as timeless as that of the thirteenth-century Cistercians.

I also think that I have been wrong to conclude that growth in God necessitates a prolonged evolution toward greater and greater solitude. The solitude is necessary, but so, too, is there a real need for social sharing. During college and after I felt a need for a greater solitude as a counterbalance to the turbulence of college life in general and specifically college life in the sixties. But now that I have to some degree swung the pendulum to the other end I find that I am not a hermit. Perhaps I am just homesick. I miss old friends.

February 3, 1976, Nagoya

This past month has not been a good one for me. In fact, since I decided to leave Japan I have been in a negative phase. At first I thought that this meant that I should reverse my decision to leave, but prospects for staying on here are not so heartening either. I've a suspicion that my spiritual state is more certainly prompting my desire to leave than any form of intellectual satisfaction or intrigue with returning to the States.

Usually there is a definite relationship for me between spiritual practice and spiritual benefit. I expect a pay-off for my self-effort. I think I have come to the end of that pleasing cycle. The distance that I feel from God this month has turned pleasing routines, such as reading Merton, sitting, or listening to sacred music, into hollow experiences.

God is no longer pleasing me. I say this in a selfish manner because I think that it is the root of my problem. I have come up against the problem that I have envisioned a Christian who practices zazen to encounter. I am counting too much upon personal efforts to win for me heavenly rewards. I have to realize that spiritual practice is not intended for me, but that it is for God. If I do all the things that have previously garnered grace for me and get nothing, then I just have to realize that the whole purpose of those efforts was not to further glorify myself.

To continue to do things pleasing to God and get no reward is one of the irrational "musts" of Christian life. I need to place further faith in the darkness. But it ain't easy. I can see how disillusionment with prayer can turn one away from Christ.

A Letter from Father Thomas

February 14, Spencer

Your spiritual state seems to be the normal development of your efforts up to now. You say: "If I do all the things that have previously garnered grace for me and get nothing, then I just have to realize that the whole purpose of those efforts was not intended to further glorify myself." That is a very precious insight. But with the same conditional clause beginning, there is another conclusion that is also very important, which is—there is no direct connection between cause and effect in regard to spiritual effort. You have to depend more on God now and less on your own efforts, without giving up those efforts. As long as you were obtaining results, you could not help but depend on those efforts. To really begin to depend on God for everything is the new level of growth that the Holy Spirit is evidently calling you to now; and so the former results of your efforts have to cease. You have to experience the dichotomy between what seems to be the same kind of efforts you made before and the very different results which you are now getting.

This is a moment of spiritual growth which always involves a profound change of attitude or disposition. Instead of looking for results, you must now look for God alone and what pleases him. You make the efforts and let God decide what the results will be. This will enable him in time to give you far more than your efforts could ever obtain. Wait on God, be patient, and persevere in your good efforts, leaving the results entirely to God. True love, as it deepens, does not look for the reward, but at the joy of serving God for his own sake.

I don't think it matters much whether you stay in Japan or come home. Your spiritual state is going to be the same. I would just caution you not to decide to change your plans just because you feel differently. In your letter you state explicitly that "my spiritual state is more certainly prompting my actions than any form of intellectual satisfaction or intrigue." You might review your motives for changing your plan about staying in Japan. Make sure your change in plans is not based solely on this change in your spiritual state, from which you would naturally tend to look around for some escape. Of the three reasons you give in the first part of your letter for leaving Japan, the desire to return to a contemplative community in the United States and homesickness were really not substantial. The first one, that you "have gathered most of the information" you came seeking was not impressive either. It sounded a little like a rationalization.

However, I know you have by now reviewed the whole situation a second time, and maybe you have come up with serious reasons for leaving Japan. If you have not, you might try this. Make up your mind that you will feel the way you do now for some time to come, more or less, and that you will feel the same no matter where you go; then make a decision about Japan and whether there are enough reasons to change your original plan.

I wish I could share with you face to face. I know how acute this kind of suffering can be, but it is only because God is hugging you extra tight.

February 24, Nagoya

Thank you for your letter of February 14, it has helped me to feel that you are with me and understand my situation. Often I think that the greatest suffering is simply not knowing where I stand in my journey. Your letter was reassuring.

Though my future plans remain uncertain, I think I now have a clearer grasp of the roots of my confusion. If you recall, last July I had a rewarding sesshin at Father Lassalle's retreat house. Although that was the time I began questioning the value of enlightenment, it was also the occasion of my most interesting spiritual experience to date. After that sesshin I returned for another, several weeks later, but could not bring myself to sit for seven more days. At that time my rationale was similar in kind to my reasons for leaving Japan. I felt that I knew enough not to need a further immersion in the world of leg pain. I remember at that time being dissatisfied with this reason, but nevertheless I latched onto it and fled.

Since that time I have had an increasingly anticlimactic feeling about both my being in Japan and my spiritual life. Since that big July sesshin "pay-off," I have had few experiences with which to glorify myself. In late December I went to a sesshin at Antai-ji but also left early. There I really did have trouble with the circulation in my left leg; however I can also remember being anxious for an excuse to get out of the sesshin. I think it is true therefore that my disgruntlement over not getting spiritual pay-offs has paralleled my disenchantment with Japan.

I have read your advice that it doesn't matter much "whether I stay in Japan or come home," and I think I understand what you are saying. Consequently I have been trying to recall just what were my thoughts for the future this last fall before all this turmoil erupted. My plans after leaving my teaching commitment have always been vague. I believe I had thought some about spending at least the summer and fall at Oshida's farm, traveling through Southeast Asia, returning home for a bit, and then perhaps going on to India. My interest in Southeast Asia and India is not well founded. It would be fascinating to see what is going on between religions in these areas, but I am not vitally interested. In fact, I continue to have no clear idea of what to do next. I suppose it would be best if I keep in close touch and try not to make any hasty decisions.

In the immediate future I plan to do a short sesshin at Antai-ji. This will be my first foray since the late December sesshin. I am going partly because I feel a need to do a long sit, but also because a year ago today I would not have allowed myself to go so long (close to three months) without an intensive retreat of one form or other. As you can see I am trying to run myself more and more by remote control. As the pay-offs decrease, I am trying to do what I would have done before when the pay-offs were more plentiful, giving less thought to what I want and more thought to what pleases God. This is easier said than done.

The greatest suffering is not knowing where I am spiritually. There *is* a welcome solace in realizing that I have now to experience a lack of pay-off for my efforts. I do see the need for a whole new disposition to arise. And it is a great assurance to know that you understand what I am going through.

Amidst all this I feel less interested in pursuing the Zen–Christian questions that have heretofore driven me. I know better than to say that I've got all the answers covered. Rather what I sense is that my personal questions and those of the Zen–Christian encounter are no longer the same, if they ever really were. Under these circumstances, I suppose it would be wise not to do anything too hastily for a while.

A Letter from Father Thomas

March 14, Spencer

I think you are wise not to do anything hastily for a while. By all means keep in close touch with me. As for your plans, summer and fall at Oshida's sounds like a good idea. Take one thing at a time. After Oshida, a visit to your home would be good, and then you can decide on your trip to Southeast Asia and India.

In your letter you sound as though you have resigned yourself well to getting along without the pay-offs. That really is the big thing right now. Follow your schedule of sitting and reading as closely as you did when they were more interesting and rewarding.

I would like to hear more of what you are doing with your mind during the time of sitting. In your situation, I think that giving one of the sittings of say twenty minutes or half-an-hour to the practice of the interior presence of God, using a single word as your focus of attention, as pointed out in *The Cloud of Unknowing*, could be very helpful.

Δ

March 28, Nagoya

Last weekend I went up to Father Oshida's farm. There I ran across a young American woman I had previously met at Antai-ji. We spent a pleasant weekend together during which I learned something of her experience in the East.

Like so many of the foreign seekers I have met in Japan, Molly is neither Christian nor Buddhist, yet she has come to Japan to do Zen meditation. She left her family several years ago to go to India. There she sought gurus, took drugs, became sick, and wandered. She was suspicious of organized religion yet eager to find a deeper peace for herself. Her parents worried. She did not go home for several years. Unlike most, Molly persevered in her searching. She made myriad mistakes, she said, with drugs, sex, and even the wrong gurus, yet she continued in her searching. In Japan, Molly came to Antai-ji where she now scratches a living teaching English while doing that temple's twice-monthly sesshin.

Molly has come to the East to find meaning in her life, risked everything, and triumphed. She is all the stronger for it. My hunch is that the great majority of Western seekers in the East are seeking answers to psychological problems wrapped in spiritual guise. For them, meditation is therapy. This has also been true for Molly (as well as for me); yet at some point the psychological problems have been largely resolved and the quest has become spiritual. Molly has come out of the free-wheeling hippie-cum-seeker whirl and found herself in meditation. She is perhaps more disciplined in her ways than the Trappist monk who has a cloister and the Benedictine Rule to buttress him. She is a principled contemplative and has come upon those principles through her own inner discovery.

Molly was in Bangladesh a short time ago. There she was gripped by the suffering of the people of that stricken nation and asked what she could do to help. They told her that they didn't need any money: it always seemed to get lost. They didn't need a whole lot of equipment either: it easily fell into disrepair and no one there knew how to fix it. What they did need were caring people to help take the dying off of the street, to live on next to nothing, and to offer their energy to those whose energy was just about gone. Molly took their advice and dug in to help. Several months later she helped the son of a man who runs an orphanage get a visa out of Bangladesh (apparently a difficult task) to come to Japan for medical training. The reason why Molly was at Takamori was to arrange a place for her Bangladeshi friend to stay while she continued to work on his entry into medical school.

Molly was recently in South Korea where she went to learn about the Zen situation and wound up staying for a three-month sesshin. She first heard about Zen in South Korea through a young westerner who passed through Kyoto. He had come from Song Kwang Sa, a large monastery with over a hundred monks in the rugged highlands of central South Korea. He told her that the monastery was run by one of the two great Zen masters in South Korea (apparently there is a distinction between Zen master and great Zen master in South Korea) and followed a rhythm of three months of sesshin, three months of work and travel, three months of sesshin and so on.

This last weekend I had a chance to talk with Father Oshida about my future plans. He urged me to spend some time soon on a long retreat. This could mean anything from a solid Zen monastic sitting schedule or living in an Indian ashram, to entering a Trappist novitiate as long as it was a thoroughgoing experience that would help me to secure a solid spiritual foundation.

In discussing the monastic commitment, Father Oshida argued that one's call is absolute; whereas, the law is relative. He feels that a person called to the monastery can also be called out of the monastery to do what he can for others. Along with Father Oshida, I believe that one of the problems of Western monastic life may be the entrenched superordinance of the law over one's call. My hunch is that monastic law has often worked against God's call in keeping monks within the cloister. Couldn't there be a legitimate call for Western Boddhisattvas[1] who, after undergoing monastic training, go out to help lay people in their spiritual journeys? And what about a whole series of experiments that would allow lay people to be monks for days, weeks, even years? Of course my interest in these new contemplative experiments is personal, for now I am interested in finding a contemplative home. I will be looking for places like that of Oshida in Southeast Asia, but I hope that a place like his can eventually come about in the United States.

You asked about my daily meditations. My morning sitting practice begins now with the reading of a few Psalms or a chapter from *The Cloud of Unknowing*. I then sit for a period of forty to fifty minutes. The first twenty minutes of the sitting is usually spent counting breaths, then concentrating

---

1. Enlightened beings who dedicate themselves to helping others attain liberation.

on each breath, until the "Lord Have Mercy" prayer emerges. This is then gradually adapted to "Lord" or "God," as the other words become heavy and burdensome, and the one word becomes the focus for the rest of my sitting. This word drifts in and out with my concentration, and may even drop away itself so that I am not focusing on anything. In the evening I need a longer settling down period, so usually before sitting I listen to a quiet piece of music or just lie down in the dark.

A Letter from Father Thomas

April 22, Spencer

I am glad that your sitting practice continues and I think that your method is good. Perhaps you could settle down a little quicker in counting breaths as time goes on and be satisfied with a single word, as *The Cloud* recommends. With that method one is constantly flirting with deep silence. You sink down, and things begin to get real quiet and then, for no apparent reason, you get shoved out.

There are three kinds of thoughts, and accordingly three different responses, which are appropriate in contemplative meditation. Superficial thoughts that the imagination grinds out because of its natural propensity for perpetual motion should be treated like the weather which you just have to accept. The important thing is not to pay any attention to them. They are like the noise in the street which floats through the window of an apartment where two people are carrying on a conversation. Their attention is firmly directed to each other, but they cannot avoid hearing the noise. Sometimes they reach a point where they don't notice it at all. At other times the honking of the horns may distract them momentarily. It would be useless to get in the elevator and go downstairs and tell the people on the street to shut up. One would then have to discontinue the conversation, and you might never be able to take it up where you left off. The only reasonable attitude is to put up with the noise and pay as little attention to it as possible. In this way you give as much of your individual attention as circumstances allow to the one with whom you are conversing.

The second kind of thought occurs when you get interested in something that is happening in the street. A brawl breaks out and attracts your curiosity. This is the kind of thought that calls for a gentle resistance. Here is where returning gently to the sacred word is a means of getting back to the general loving attention you are offering to God. It is important not to be annoyed with yourself if you get caught in these interesting thoughts. Sometimes a brilliant idea will present itself which you want to look at just long enough so that you won't forget to think about it afterward. That is a great mistake, because any annoyance or any curiosity that you give in to is another thought, and that takes you farther out of the interior silence, which is the proximate goal of the meditation. Silence is always going to be relative. You will be flirting with deep silence most of the time. It is an exercise of waiting, a fulfillment of the Gospel precept of the Lord to watch and pray. It is an exercise of endless patience—which leads me to the third kind of thoughts.

Any form of contemplative meditation sets off the dynamics of interior purification, whether you look upon it as a purification of the nervous system, as the Hindus do, or as a purification of the faculties, as St. John of the Cross and most of the Christian tradition present the process. This process is a kind of divine psychotherapy. It takes place however without retraumatizing our psyche by remembering traumatic events of the past and is designed to empty out the unconscious. According to Maharishi,[2] it is the deep rest that comes with Transcendental Meditation which releases pockets of stress in the nervous system. These emerge in the form of a strong thought or emotion during meditation, which tosses you out of the deep tranquility you might have been enjoying. However you want to conceptualize this process, there is no doubt that it is very real. The unconscious is full of all kinds of junk, and it all has to come out before our spirit can be fully united to God both in itself and in its faculties.

It is almost impossible to tell what thoughts come from this source, especially when they are very vague and not too strong, and which come from our own inveterate tendency to reflect on ourselves, even when we are enjoying deep tranquility and silence. I suspect that it is not so much the thoughts in the unconscious, but our unconscious attachment to *possess* which is the real thing that has to be purified by God.

---

2.   Maharishi Mahesh Yogi, the founder of Transcendental Meditation

In any case, it is obvious that these thoughts are a good thing, so we should not lament or grieve by being distracted by them. Everything that happens then in contemplative meditation should be accepted without judging what is good or bad for us, but treating each kind of thought in the appropriate manner. The first kind is to be ignored. The second and third require the gentle return of our attention toward our original intent to go to God in the depth of our being. The sacred word is just a vehicle, a means of moving in that direction; or rather of letting go in order to fall in that direction (or rise in that direction, if you prefer a different image).

I am very interested in your own thoughts about monastic reforms. There is no doubt that some new forms need to be introduced, perhaps not in the existing monastic structures of the ancient orders, but at least beside them or near them or with some kind of guidance from them.

I think some kind of moderate monastic lifestyle that would incorporate the essential values could be instituted in a noncanonical way, if some traditional monastery would agree to accept the spiritual guidance of it for a few years. My experience is that after three or four months people in our residency program begin to enter the specifically monastic form of purification. Since this takes several years, it is important that they stay long enough to complete the process, or at least get a good head-start on it, or leave before it begins. I've noticed that most of our residents get a little restless after three or four months. If they were going to stay longer, they would really need a formation program, something that we would find difficult to provide from a practical point of view, given the fact that we already have one novitiate in the community for permanent members. I am inclined to think that this sort of monastic training would have to be in a separate place on the property or maybe the permanent novitiate should be in a separate place; or perhaps the novices would be more willing to accept long-term residents of two or three years rather than our short-term variety.

I think it might be better to allow young people to evolve outside of canonical structures for a while. You would need a core group, and they would have to decide what they could handle in the way of temporary vocations. To lead the monastic life for a few days or a few weeks is quite different from leading it for six months or longer. But it would be a good thing to provide an experience for everyone.

As you can see, I am putting a good deal of thought on this too. I look forward to talking to you about it at greater length when you get back to the States.

Δ

April 26, Nagoya

Through unforeseen circumstances my travel plans are approaching final form. Two weeks ago I was in the midst of planning a long Southeast Asia trip that would have taken me back home in time for Christmas. This changed, however, when I got a call from my older sister, Anne, in Chicago informing me that she planned to marry in August and that she hoped I could come home for the wedding. Things began to fall in place and I came up with the following plan. This summer I will visit South Korea, Taiwan, Hong Kong, and Thailand, all by the end of July, then take a flight home to the States. I don't know what I will do after the wedding, though this need to spend time in a contemplative environment continues to make sense to me. I am beginning to feel like a pregnant cat looking for a place to give birth to its kittens. I will go to Southeast Asia and learn what I can about the religious scene in those countries, but now I feel that I am ripe for retreat, maybe a Trappist monastery.

I am moving away now from Zen–Christian questions and becoming more interested in how the church is living with communism. I speak specifically of the deteriorating political situations in Korea and Thailand. And what is happening in Vietnam?

As I write letters to the various people I wish to contact, I am intrigued by how I phrase my interests and my goals. I have been saying that my Southeast trip has two goals. One is to further pursue the interreligious dialogue by seeing what is going on in these countries. Two is to learn how the church is or has or will have to adapt to communism in the areas where it is, has, or will be threatened. I also have found myself describing my role as one who is hoping to influence fundamental change in the church. Now as I look at copies of these letters, I wonder if these are my real motives? I *am* interested in all this. Still I think that this "living with communism" question may be really a veiled inquiry into the personal question "How shall I live?"

May 1, Nagoya

My summer plans have become as clear as I think they are going to be. I will leave for South Korea on June 14, traveling there by ferry from a port in southern Japan. The ferry will go to the port of Pusan in southern South Korea where I hope to spend a day with a Protestant missionary who lives there. During the eight days I will have in South Korea, I hope to spend several days visiting the Zen monasteries, particularly Song Kwang Sa. After taking a ferry back to Japan on June 22, I will return by train to Nagoya and then go on up by train to Tokyo for a flight to Taiwan on June 24. A friend here has given me the names of some people to contact in Taipei. They are priests on the theology faculty at the Jesuit-run Fu-Jen University. Also in Taiwan I hope to visit the Lion's Head mountain group of Buddhist monasteries just south of Taiwan, and take a trip along the mountainous East–West highway. Around July 1, I will head for Hong Kong where the only contacts I now have are at the Trappist monastery on Lantau Island and with a young seminarian.

On July 10 or so I will head out to Thailand where I have fewer contacts still, but by that time I think some itinerary for Thailand will have developed. I plan to leave Bangkok in late July and fly to Hong Kong where I will board a charter flight to the States on July 30.

June 8. Nagoya

One month ago I wrote a letter to Aelred Graham in England asking him if he knew of any Buddhist monks who might be willing to speak with me when I arrived in Bangkok. Dom Graham, who had traveled through Thailand several years before, gave me the name of an Englishman who is a Hinayana Buddhist monk. When I wrote this monk, Phra Khantipalo, I told him about my interest in Buddhism and Christianity. His reply came from Sri Lanka where he had recently moved.

A Letter from Phra Khantipalo

June 1, Forest Hermitage. Udanattakele, Kandy

Your letter of May 15 has just reached me and I am not sure whether this reply will reach you in time before you set off on your travels. If you are coming to Sri Lanka I shall be happy to see you at this address where I will be staying for the next year.

In Thailand you should go to the Mahamakut Buddhist Book-shop and World Fellowship of Buddhists for information on whom to meet. I do not know exactly who is where now and so cannot give more detailed advice upon whom you should meet.

"Dialogue," a word which has suddenly become fashionable in Western Christianity—though not in favor I suppose with the majority of Christians for the last nineteen centuries—has always been a part of the Indian religious scene. Perhaps it was in fact a reason for the lack of rigidity there. The Buddha himself had numerous encounters with those of other views and his discourses on these subjects are now all available in English translation. On our side then, there has always been openness to others. It is heart-ening to see that this is happening also in Christianity.

You mentioned about meditation—and I have met both with Dom Aelred and Father Merton in this connection. However, it does not seem to have been realized by these good teachers that components of one religion cannot be borrowed and grafted onto another. I remember an interesting talk with Father Merton on Satipatthana, the Foundations of Mindfulness, which are basic to all Buddhist practices. When they are fully practiced there is just the experience of physical and mental phenomena arising and passing away—and all ideas, even of religion, even of Buddhism, have vanished. When practiced sufficiently this leads to the pene-tration of momentariness of all experience, with the cutting off of all views and conceit, which is basically "I am." Cutting off all views means ceasing to believe anything—it would mean for a Roman Catholic ceasing to believe in God, the Trinity, the Virgin Mary, the Saints, and so on, all the dogmas on which that religion is founded.

Sincere Christians, if they want to borrow from Buddhism, are in a quandary since they wish to meditate but still to hang on to their views. This can be done only part of the way. That is to say, using *samatha* (calming) techniques, the mind may be calmed, and having withdrawn from that inward purity and bliss, one may still go on believing in the tenets of one's religion—and probably see it in quite a different light as some of the great contemplatives of Christianity, like Meister Eckhardt, have. But if one approaches *Vipassana* (insight)—not of course just to practice it for a week, or even a month, but for a long time—then by the nature of its disci-pline, which is to force one to regard only what exists and to see that this is all impermanent, unsatisfactory, and ownerless (without self or soul—or void), then all views must be given up. Such a person could not cling to any views as props for his self or his ego. Having given them up, if he called himself by any name he would be a Buddhist, out of gratitude to the Buddha for having shown the truth that was there to be seen all the time, and for having rid him through his own practice—of that troublesome self, to awaken to non-self.

I cannot see many Christians being prepared to go so far, for if they do they can no longer be Christians.

It seems to me that the rigidity of Christian monasticism follows directly from a set of rigid beliefs. The Church, even now I suspect, may be suspicious of meditation because a meditator, even using samatha, may attain this deeper insight. Rigid beliefs may help to organize the masses or get the work done, but they do not allow monks to be *quiet* and *by themselves* for long periods.

Perhaps what you are really interested in is having a quiet and peaceful heart which knows directly the truth as it really is. This will be better than searching the world for "dialogue" and "adaptations of monasticism." In that case I would suggest that you find a meditation teacher in Thailand and stay with him for say, five or ten years. This is the only way to do it. And if it does happen that your "conversion" becomes unstuck, well there is no great fear or sorrow on that account. In our many lives we have surely believed all sorts of things. In this one, however, one should resolve to end all this believing, entirely to tear it out by the roots.

You can never find peace and satisfaction by traveling all over the world. It sounds all too much like the usual feverish Western search. Be quiet and stay in one place.

Δ

June 8, Nagoya

Today, just before leaving for South Korea, I have sent Phra Khantipalo the following response:

A little over two years ago I was twenty-three and a university student. I had already spent several years looking into different spiritual paths as they were becoming available here and there in the United States. In these paths I met several impressive men from the East. When, in the summer of 1974, I went to live in a Trappist monastery for three months and was baptized into the Catholic Church; it was not a denial of my experience with paths from the East. Instead it was an affirmation of what I felt was closer to home, closer to my culture.

In your warm and helpful letter, you suggest that I spend five or ten years with a meditation teacher in Thailand. Your words make sense to me and it is only the location that I find difficult to take. It is perhaps like asking a Thai boy to study Catholicism for five or ten years in Iowa.

In the intermingling of religions and cultures that is now becoming more and more commonplace, there is an awkward tension. Westerners practicing Eastern paths have difficulty reintegrating themselves and their beliefs with the culture in which they were raised. Surely the scene is ever changing but there always seems to be an unhealthy tension between foreign faith and native culture. I know that talk of home and culture can be readily disposed of through mystical retorts about a deep inner peace that allows you to be at home wherever you go. I'm in no experiential position to deny this. Still, before westerners convert to Buddhism, I wonder if they should not first take a deeper look at their more native faith.

When I first ran across Trappist monks, it was with more than the average amount of suspicion. I didn't care at all for parish priests or the authoritarian "church." However, just as I had been impressed by the wise men of the East, so too was I impressed by Trappist monks. It was true that there was much wrong and still is and will be much wrong with the monasticism and the church. But the fact that these were obviously spiritual people who had grown from roots long cultivated in my culture was decisive. Becoming a Catholic took me out of tension with my culture and made me feel more at home growing into its roots.

And now that I find myself a Catholic, I am coming up against the problems of grafting components of one religion onto another that you raise in your letter. So why am I doing zazen and running all over the East like a lost fool?

I suppose in one way that I am hedging my bets by augmenting my culture's faith with the powerful spiritual tools of the East. Yes, and this is grafting for sure. But I don't think that I am looking for new tools that might help in the creation of new Christian–Buddhist hybrids in the West. Rather I am trying to discover the heart of all religions, a heart that has become difficult to discover in the West given only the available Western tools. I am looking for a peace that is present in all religions, but happens to be piled under quite a heap of confusion in the Christian path. I think to remain a Christian I have to say that Buddhism does not transcend Christianity so much as it is able to more easily penetrate to Christianity's depth.

The Western church is in need of new tools and fresh insights that might help Christians and the church to rediscover their true nature. The grafting of East to West is like the introduction of the wheel to a culture that has forgotten that once before it had created such a tool. Once Catholics, through the aid of the East, come to know a greater depth in their faith, then too they will discover or rediscover the tools of exploration left buried and forgotten by ancient Christian voyagers and no longer need assistance from the East. I frankly believe that any great religion in existence for more than a thousand years reproduces just about every phenomena known in the history of religions. Our problem in the West is that we have largely lost access to the profound nature of our religion. Once we come to a deeper grasp of our faith then there will hopefully be an end to the amalgamation of religions that leaves us all decked out in universals yet all longing for our religious and cultural home.

So I am learning what I can while I am in the East in the hope of taking back whatever insights and tools that may be helpful for Westerners to rediscover the depth of their faith. Once both monks and lay people rediscover that depth, borrowed tools that remain out of place may simply fall away.

Part II

South Korea and Southeast Asia

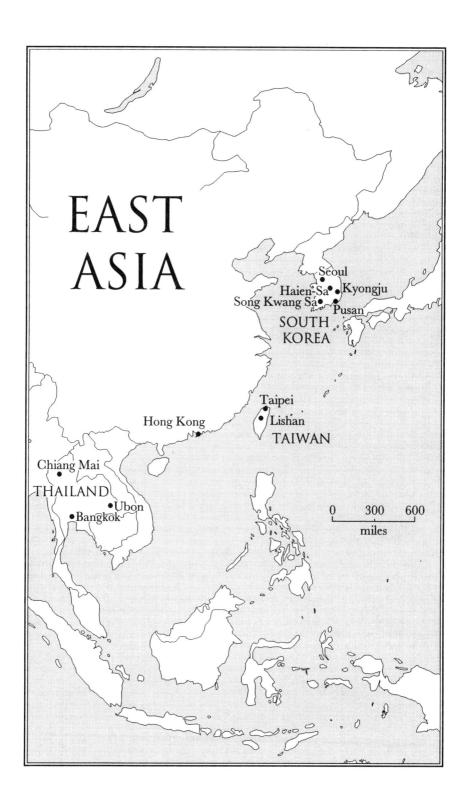

EAST
ASIA

Seoul
Haien-Sa Kyongju
Song Kwang Sa Pusan
SOUTH
KOREA

Taipei
Hong Kong Lishan
TAIWAN

Chiang Mai
THAILAND Ubon
Bangkok

0   300   600
miles

South Korea

June 15, 1976, Pusan

Five-thirty A.M. in the Pusan harbor. Our ship has been sitting in the bay since midnight, waiting for South Korea's midnight to four A.M. curfew to lift and for the customs office to open. There are a half dozen foreigners on the boat. In my cub reporter manner I have met most of them. One is an older man who said he had come to Japan a month ago from San Francisco. He arrived with his Japanese wife to attend her father's funeral. After a month with the family and mindful that his wife could not leave just yet, he is spending his time traveling about. This week South Korea. Others include two young men from Fort Wayne, Indiana, and a young woman from Livonia, Michigan. On the spur of the moment last February, the three of them decided to travel around the world. One of the men is carrying two thousand dollars in cash in his pocket, the other has a big pot belly and a T-shirt that doesn't quite cover his navel. I haven't seen much of the woman. She has apparently spent most of the journey feverishly writing letters home to family and friends.

Then there is the Peace Corps fellow who had been willing to be sent anywhere and wound up in a tuberculosis and leprosy clinic in South Korea, and the Harvard Ph.D. candidate doing research on the Korean land system. The latter told me that the only way South Korean president Park Chung Hee could be turned toward a more democratic government would be through an open threat by United States forces to leave South Korea.

The Harvard student also noted that there are few well-known Buddhist establishments in South Korean cities. This is a result of Buddhism's falling into disfavor in the 1500s. At that time all of the temples had been banished to the remote countryside. Of those temples that remained, he said there were three major monastic complexes which would be worth my while to visit. One of these is Song Kwang Sa, which I hope to see tomorrow.

I've been told that South Korea has a population of thirty-three million and that thirteen percent of these are Christians (compared to less than one percent in Japan). Most of these Christians are in the cities, where forty percent of the population resides. I hope to be met at the ship terminal by one of Pusan's American missionaries.

June 16, Pusan

There is a marvelous mystery, an eerie, almost frightening sense of bewilderment and discovery in waking up in surroundings so foreign to one's own. Sounds of the marketplace and the bustling of cars shout over the high wall and barbed wire enclosure of this one-seventh acre compound where I am staying. I am in an older house in a crowded section of Pusan, two blocks from the red-light district. I walked there last night and, in trying to find out the going rate for a rented woman, had the madame steal my shoes. This was apparently the standard procedure. Once they have you inside the shop and gazing upon their line-up of heavily perfumed bodies, they take your shoes away, which is one way of making you stay. I had a heck of a time getting them back. Only when I revealed that I had no money did they in disgruntlement return my sandals and let me go. Anyway, it is early morning in Pusan.

Yesterday Ted Hard, a Protestant missionary, picked me up at the ferry terminal and took me home to this compound where his wife served us breakfast. I talked with the two of them for a while, took an all-day stroll through the city, and in the evening jogged about the harbor with Mr. Hard. The Hards came to Pusan twenty-two years ago and raised their four children here amidst the large foreign missionary community. They are Presbyterians and take pride in the rising percentage of the population that is Christian.

South Korea was flooded by missionaries at the end of the Korean War, which helps account for the disproportionate number of churches per people in this busy, drab industrial and fishing center. There are churches everywhere, and sometimes four on a corner. Why are there so many Christians in South Korea? Some clues include: the ravaged spirit of the South Korean people from years of subservience to foreign powers, Western influence during the Korean War, and the heavy concentration of missionaries.

The town of Pusan was a poor fishing center of 100,000 people when it was abruptly bloated by over two million refugees during the Korean War. Most of these newcomers have stayed on in the now squalid, cramped, and dirty urban atmosphere. The town is on a series of hillsides facing the ocean with house upon house rising up in terraced rows. Old men sit in doorway stoops wearing white, broad-brimmed hats playing board games. Children play in the streets.

Yesterday at noon I was at the top of a tower in the center of town getting a broad view of the city when an air force jet streaked by and an air raid alert sounded. Down below me all movement on the street froze and then quickly everyone went inside. Soldiers with rifles and in camouflage dress, supported by large groups of green-capped civilians, patrolled the streets to make sure that everyone obeyed the alert. Later I learned that this air raid was a regular occurrence on the fifteenth of every month; still, at that moment, I thought I was in a rather vulnerable position for a war.

June 16, Song Kwang Sa

Sign at the entrance to Song Kwang Sa:

A HISTORY OF
SONG KWANG SA

Song Kwang Sa was constructed about 1200 years ago during the Silla Dynasty by the Meditation Master Hye Rin, an exponent of the Avatamsaka (Flower Garland) Sutra. In 1197 A.D., the National Master Bo Jo had a disciple search the entire country for the most suitable location for a spiritual cultivation site. After this monastery's selection, he moved here with many disciples and promoted the teachings of Mahayana Soen (Zen) Buddhism, reviving the Buddhism of the Koryo period. Subsequently the monastery produced sixteen National Masters and many great monks. As the monastery represents the jewel of the Buddhist monastic order, it is regarded as one of the cardinal sacred areas of Korean Buddhism.

In 1969 the monastery was organized as a Cheng Lim: a monastic center uniting all the sects of Mahayana Buddhism. Since that time a large number of monks have been fully devoting themselves to spiritual cultivation. At the International Meditation Center, Western monks are trained in traditional Mahayana Soen practices. In major cities throughout Korea, branch temples have been established for the edification of the country.

It is a cool, summer day. A river rushes in the background, a soft wind blows. I am sitting on a stoop outside the temple doors of Song Kwang Sa, a monastery nestled in a remote mountain valley of central South Korea. In the many buildings that surround the monastery's central square, a hundred devotees are sitting silently in meditation.

A young monk comes, opens the door, glances at me, then retreats. He is wearing gray pants and a gray shirt, both long and loose, and a wide-brimmed straw hat. Perhaps he has gone to inform the guestmaster.

Seven hours later. I am in a guest room heated, as in most Korean rooms, by warm air passageways under the floor. I have met the master and most of the foreign monks, and taken some notes.

This is the major monastery for meditation in South Korea. It is now undergoing a revival under one of the two great Zen masters in South Korea, Panumkunsanim. He has been a monk of Song Kwang Sa for more than forty-five years. There are more than fifteen thousand monks in South Korea and about four thousand of these are seriously involved in Zen meditation (others are scholars, clerics, and the like). The monks travel about from temple to temple, seeking out the masters who can help them in their spiritual growth.

To enter the monastery you have to go through six months of hard, physical labor, which is followed by several years as a novice. When you finally become a monk, it is assumed you are becoming one for life. There is a vow of stability, but the foreign monks told me that the vow is rendered ineffective by the belief that your mind commits you to that vow and the whole purpose of the monastic life is to get beyond your mind.

This is a remote monastery and, I am told, the monks know little outside of their Buddhism, just as the Catholic Church knew little about Buddhism fifty years ago. The master and the monks have spent most of their lives in solitude either here or in other temples. Up until a year ago the master would have stated categorically that Christianity and Buddhism are totally different. However, one of the American monks began talking to the master about the similarities in all religions and now he is said to be more open to Christianity.

The yearly schedule calls for three months of sesshin in the summer followed by three months of work and travel to other temples in the fall, sesshin for the three winter months, and then on to three months of work and travel in the spring to complete the cycle. Daily the monks rise at three (two in winter) and pursue the following schedule.

Δ

3:30 A.M.	Temple service
4:00	Sit
6:00	Breakfast
6:30	Sit
12:00	Lunch
1:00	Sit
6:30	Dinner
7:00	Sit
7:30	Temple service
8:00	Bed

Some of the monks are now involved in a three-year sesshin that started six months ago, others are doing the three-month sesshin. A skeleton crew keeps the place in order. In the meditation hall they sit for fifty minutes then walk for ten minutes. The person in charge of the sittings is not too strict. Meditators are allowed to slouch and even fall asleep, occasionally some tip over on their side.

I am told that it is prestigious to have foreign monks in the monastery. The master has reserved one small area of the temple grounds for the five foreign monks and two nuns. The nuns are an oddity in that there are no Korean nuns at this temple. They are allowed to stay, however, through the courtesy of the master. The foreign monks include two Americans from California, two Frenchmen, and a New Zealander. All of them did some knocking about, mostly in Thailand, before coming here. The New Zealander was the first to arrive, two years ago. He was pointed this way by an organization in Bangkok called the World Fellowship of Buddhists. The Frenchmen are the most traveled. One has been with a roshi in Paris, Sasaki Roshi in southern California, and two years with Yamada Mumon Roshi in Kyoto. The other knows Chinese and some Korean and interprets for the other foreigners. Language is a major problem for the foreigners as are the great number of rituals that need to be learned.

One of the Americans, a young fellow named Billy, is doing a three-year sesshin. It is hard to describe him. He is like a helium balloon about to float away. This goes for all of these foreigners. They have been doing so much sitting that there is an ethereal quality to them. They were happy to see me, another foreigner, but their meditation practice has them so zonked out that it was difficult to relate to them. They seemed so distant, so transparent, so far gone.

Δ

June 17, Song Kwang Sa

Song Kwang Sa is a Shangri-La. The rhythm of this monastery seems to have pulsed for an eternity. As I passed my two days here it seemed as if I had journeyed to another planet. Walking the hills, passing hidden hermitages, returning to the deserted temple grounds in late afternoon when everyone was sitting, I felt like I had passed through the twilight into another world. They are about such an otherworldly business.

The evening before I left, along with several of the foreign monks, I had a chance to have an audience with Panumkunsanim. The master, a lithe, energetic man in his fifties, sat bright-eyed in one corner of his room, fingering his prayer beads, and attentive to all who were around him. When the opportunity came I asked the following question. "Since every enlightenment is identical to that of the Buddha, why is it that different masters act differently and some even appear to lack compassion?" Panumkunsanim shelved my question saying that the answer was detailed and he would go into it with me later, but we never did get back to it. Later one of the foreign monks, who had heard the master answer that same question before, told me that Panumkunsanim would probably have said either that a master who is not compassionate is not yet fully enlightened, or that a master who acts without compassion may be doing it for an overriding spiritual reason that will eventually benefit his student. This latter explanation, though it makes sense, is the elastic clause that has been used by many supposed Eastern sages in the West to engage in immoral or illicit activities.

June 17, Seoul

I am in Seoul this evening. I had planned to take the long dirt road to Haien-Sa, the second of the three great Buddhist monasteries in South Korea, but the trip would have taken too long, so I have decided to go north, see Seoul, and then approach Haien-Sa from the other side, via a paved road.

This is a nervous city, disturbed by constant threats of invasion from North Korea and the preparedness exhortations of President Park. The military guards on the outskirts of Seoul boarded my bus looking for infiltrators from the North. They asked several passengers for their identification, saluted all of us twice, and left. There are sand bags piled outside major buildings downtown.

June 18, Seoul

Boarding a bus that seemed to be under instructions to evacuate the city, I rode along as it engorged and disgorged passengers at a breakneck pace all the way to the city's outskirts. There I got off and looked up a middle-aged Irish parish priest I contacted yesterday. We had lunch together and chatted for several hours about the Catholic situation in South Korea. The following is what I learned from Father Tom Cleery.

"Why is Christianity growing so rapidly in South Korea?" I asked. A first reason, responded Father Cleery, is President Park's strong stand against the Communists. The military and the government strongly encourage the people to be religious because the Communists are opposed to religion. This does not mean that all should become Christians (Park himself is a Buddhist) but that they should embrace some religion. A second reason for Christianity's growth, Cleery related, is the state of South Korea's other religions. Buddhism is in a sectarian shambles. Shamanism and animism are growing more and more obsolete but still hold sway over a large number of the rural poor. A third reason is the devil in Christianity. The Korean nature religions are built around a struggle between good and evil, the divine and the devil, and a pantheism with which the Catholic theology works particularly well. A fourth reason is the economic example of America and the presence of American troops. Christianity is naturally associated with the West. A final reason is the postwar flood of missionaries into Korea. Father Cleery pointed out that there are probably more churches in Korea now than the Christian population warrants.

"What will happen to Christianity in South Korea if the North overruns the South?" So far as Father Cleery knows there are no contingency plans. All indications are that there would be a violent war and the South Koreans don't plan to lose.

"How important is the Sun Myung Moon movement in South Korea?" The Moon movement is big and growing, Cleery replied. This is largely due to its firm stance against communism. Though not overtly connected to the government, the Moon people receive a great deal of government cooperation. For example, when they hold rallies, they always get Seoul's largest pavilion and police assistance. In contrast, when the Catholics last year sought the same pavilion, for a rally marking the fiftieth anniversary of the death of Catholic Korean martyrs, they were denied that pavilion and given no police assistance at a smaller site. The Moon movement is also enormously wealthy due in large part to tithing and government cooperation in Moon's seven business enterprises.

The Moon theology is a mixture of pagan and Christian ideas built around Moon and his second wife as the Divine Parents and Moon as tantamount to the second coming of Christ. In Korea these beliefs play right into the older, animistic beliefs of the people. In the United States, Moon's broad appeal appears to come more from the disciplined, caring father figure he portrays. He offers his disciples instructions on what to do with their lives and how to do it. Apparently many young Americans are clamoring for just this sort of discipline and approval.

June 19, Haien-Sa

Today I have traveled for several hours by bus to the remote monastic complex of Haien-Sa, the second of the three major Buddhist monastic complexes in South Korea and the last one I will be visiting. Though somewhat more accessible than Song Kwang Sa, Haien-Sa retains the atmosphere of an eternal, transcendent world. Again I am in the misty mountain scenery which is the inspiration of so many Oriental paintings. Again there are the precipitous hills, rushing streams, shaven-headed and gray-robed monks. The monastery consists of thirteen residence clusters in the hills surrounding the ancient temple buildings. In the building where I am staying there is no plumbing and little electricity. The kitchen is a large, rammed-earth space under the shrine room. There old women labor over huge black kettles hung in a large fireplace, while water diverted from a stream rushes through one end of the room. It seems again that these people and this monastery have been going on like this for an eternity.

Though there are both monks and nuns here, Haien-Sa seems to be more of a museum than a vibrant monastery. It is more accessible for the tourist trade and apparently there is not a master here of the same renown as the one at Song Kwang Sa. Nevertheless, it is a special place. After scouting the temple grounds, I returned to my room next to the shrine room and fell asleep. I was awakened by the unearthly chanting beginning in the room next door. Deep voices, bells, and gongs—and quickly I tried to figure out where I was and what century we were in.

South Korea is ripe for a James Michener novel. A tale of changing people, told perhaps from the timeless view of an aging Haien-Sa monk. He could weave together the lives of the soldier here for a weekend of retreat, the peasant in the village that supports the temple, the city-tourist out for a few days of relaxation. Each life juxtaposed with the imposing statement of transcendence that is this and so many ancient temples.

After two days and a night at Haien-Sa, I am pushing on for Kyongju, the ancient capital of South Korea. I wish I could say more about these great monastic complexes, but they are rendering me inarticulate. All I can do is mumble Shangri-La and eternity. They are such profound witnesses to the transcendent in our lives.

June 20, Kyongju

Mealtime at the cheap inn. I have twelve different dishes before me, not one of which I recognize, so I am going about sampling and hoping I don't hit upon the hot foods before I feel full. No chance. Korean food has been burning away my mouth since the day I arrived. The peppers especially make me feel like a dragon.

Today I have taken a long bus trip to Kyongju on the southeastern coast. This is the ancient capital of an old Korean kingdom. The government seems to be in a hurry to turn Kyongju into a high-class tourist trap. This makes for an unnatural juxtaposition of expensive buildings and village shacks. All South Korea seems to be this way—an advanced, poor country, leaping ahead in some areas, primitive in others.

Several things happened on the bus ride here. At the terminal in Haien-Sa, the bus driver sought to increase his earnings by illegally loading people into the aisles. Once we got out on the road, he kept an eye out for police cars and inhospitable tollgate operators. Whenever the bus went through a tollgate or the bus driver spotted a police car, he commanded everyone in the aisles to squat down low so they wouldn't be seen. He had an accomplice in the female conductor who blew her whistle frantically just before the police cars passed. Quite a scene resulted and recurred two or three times an hour. There I was reading a newspaper and all of a sudden some young fellow was on my lap and somebody's groceries were pushing my knees against the seat in front of me. The police car passed and everything abruptly returned to normal only to have everyone crash to the floor again fifteen minutes later.

Intermittent with these rushes to the floor were the hawking pleas from the vendors who slipped onto the bus at every stop along the road. These people, mostly young boys selling candy or old, very intense women selling ice cream, stood over me for long minutes awaiting my weak submission to their hard sell. As a "wealthy" foreigner, I attracted a crowd of them and when I refused to buy I seemed to get a lot of sarcasm as they stomped off of this bus to await the next one.

There were also hawkers who stayed on the bus. Once one of the little boys riding in the back got up and started handing out little pieces of paper with a few words on them to every passenger. It was apparently a plea for money, for soon he had his arm around my neck and his hand out. This guy was followed by another fellow, also riding the bus, who gave all of us a two-minute demonstration of the benefits of the pencil cases he was selling. These on-bus vendors must work certain routes, getting off at one stop and going back to the last. Certainly they are entertaining, but their hard sell only underlines the grim economic situation in South Korea where the per capita annual income is under four hundred dollars.

This evening, walking the streets of Kyongju and in between the persistent offers of a woman for the night (I must look like any other G.I. in civvies), I watched the people in their shops, all glued to their television sets. The whole town seemed to turn to the "tube" around seven o'clock, though some continued to work. I saw a two-man shovel. One fellow digs and pushes and the other in front of him pulls on a rope tied just above the spade. A few women were cleaning clothes in the river. And there was the boy who had tied together the front and back paws of his dog in separate bundles so he could sling his pet across the back fender of his bike and carry him around.

June 21, Pusan

I woke up at five in the morning and took in a temple in Kyongju before heading south to Pusan. I am now ensconced in an eight-dollar-a-night "luxury" hotel at a beach resort a bit north of Pusan. This is my splurge. My budget allows for fifteen dollars of "mad money," so here I am, sleeping in the afternoon.

An hour ago I risked an "I'll have what the other guy is having" experience in a restaurant and was treated to raw eel which seemed to be stuffed with chips of cement. So now I have repaired to my hotel's dining room where I am paying more but at least I will have some idea of what I am getting. My forays into Korean food have been uniformly disappointing. Then again, I'm making little effort to speak the language or travel normal tourist routes. I get what I deserve.

After watching countless mothers wash their clothes in a nearby stream, I asked about the hotel's laundry service. When they quoted me a high price for the service I declined, but then the maid, who has been mothering me, scooped up my clothes and soon I saw her out at the stream. Two hours later she returned and hung the clothes all over my room (I paid her what I could.) So now my clothes are stream-clean.

June 22, Pusan

Damp clothes in tow, I am heading for a ferry. Tonight I will travel back to Japan and the next day take a train up to Nagoya, stop for a few hours to see friends, then on to Tokyo to catch a flight to Taiwan on June 24.

... *10*
Taiwan

Though it may be a bit early for such requests, let it be known that I wish to die on Singapore Airlines. Never have I had such a pleasantly inebriating flight. First there was the pre-meal juice (champagne), and they offered seconds. Then came the red or white wine with the filet mignon at lunchtime (seconds and thirds available on the wine). Finally, cross my heart, cognac or Tia Maria. Well I took two of the first, two of the second and one of the third, and come customs time was very happy to be in Taiwan or anyplace else.

The good times continued as I paid a mere dollar for a three-mile ride from the airport to the city (cabs in Taipai are reportedly the cheapest in the world). Then I got a room at the International House for five bucks including an air-conditioner (it is humid and the thermometer is at 95° F outside). This string of luck went on as the hotel clerk said they would wash all of my clothes for twenty-five cents.

I switched into shorts and sandals, hopped onto a number of buses and checked out the city. I returned from my tour, had dinner at the hotel for seventy-five cents, and read through the guidebook.

Unlike South Korea, where an apparently corrupt and domineering government keeps the people fearful of both the Communists from the North and the unpredictable, authoritarian actions of their own leaders, Taiwan appears to have a stable and efficient government. There is indeed a desire to recapture mainland China and also to defend the country from Communist attack. Still I do not feel here the xenophobia that was so tangible in Seoul.

I am told that Confucianism is the primary philosophy of the people while Buddhism and Taoism are the chief religions, though the three are usually lumped together as the "Chinese religions." Of the sixteen million people on the island, there are 600,000 Christians, half of them Catholic. I hope to learn more about the religious situation in Taiwan tomorrow when I will meet with several of the Jesuits on the faculty of theology at Taipei's Fu-Jen University.

June 25, Taipei

I have just returned from a full day of talks at Fu-Jen University. In the morning I spoke with Father Mark Fang, the rector. In the afternoon I saw Father Gutheinz, who is very interested in the Chinese religions. At the end of the day I sat down with Father Matthew Chen, a Chinese priest recently expelled from his teaching position in a seminary in South Vietnam. The major discussion topics were the Chinese religions, and the state of Catholicism in Taiwan.

The Chinese religions include Taoism, Confucianism, and Buddhism. After the discussions today I understand that Taoism roughly compares to negative theology in that it is devoid of dogmatic principles. As a popular religion it is animistic and mystical, laying special emphasis on reaching ultimate harmony, balance, yin-yang equilibrium in one's life and in the universe. As a religious philosophy, a transcendent wisdom, Taoism draws from its wisdom books, which include the *Tao te Ching* (sayings of Lao-Tzu) and the *I Ching* (that tells one's fortune), as well as from the movement meditation, T'ai Chi; Taoism exists today as a pantheistic popular religion and a religious philosophy. Taoists speak of attaining immortality through eating certain foods, acquiring magical powers, and leading a balanced life. There are Taoist monasteries where monks learn from a master how to acquire magical powers (In Korea, one of the foreign monks at Song Kwang Sa told me that the Taoists who lived in the mountains thereabouts lived on a mixture of pine needle and soybean powder while they worked to develop the concentration necessary to perform superhuman feats like jumping over trees). The Taoist literature is highly regarded in present-day Taiwan, I was told, but Taoism as a faith has few serious devotees.

A second Chinese religion is Confucianism, which compares roughly to Catholic moral theology and is said to be more of a philosophy than a religion. Confucianism says nothing about an after-life. Instead it seeks to have the people first put themselves in order, then their families, their state, their country, and finally the world. From what I learned, Confucianism is a system of moral behavior that has at its root a deep respect for family ties. It is the core of the Chinese social system. In early China, Confucianism was something like a positive complement to Taoism's negative theology, together they framed the moral and religious life of the people.

When Buddhism, the third Chinese religion, came to China around the time of the birth of Christ, it was swallowed nearly whole by Confucianism and Taoism. Buddhism gave to the other two a greater ascetic discipline and a more articulate theology. However, Confucianism and Taoism were not willing to take on the negative view that life was suffering and everything was illusion. The Chinese have a positive, joyful attitude toward life that seems to have changed Buddhism so that in its Chinese form there is greater emphasis placed upon the Taoist's yin-yang balance and less on the belief that life is suffering. Buddhism gave the Chinese their first exposure to the idea of reincarnation and thus gave them a broader philosophical grasp of an after-life.

The Chinese religion is an amalgamation of these three faiths. There are now and have been myriad mixtures of the three. Chinese Buddhism is filled with Taoist ideas and Confucian morality. In a rough sense Confucianism deals with one's political, moral life; Taoism with one's private life; and Buddhism with the after-life. Confucianism is a set of ethical principles, whereas Buddhism and, to some extent, Taoism have specific religious practices. Together the three religions radiate a positive, joyful attitude toward life, a sense of balance and a feeling of eternity, which, I am told, are primary traits of the Chinese people.

Regarding the state of the Catholic Church in Taiwan, the priests at the theologate told me that after the takeover of mainland China by the Communists in 1949 Taiwan experienced an influx of refugees including a disproportionately large number of Christians. This caused the Catholic population to increase from 15,000 to 200,000 by 1960. Taiwan is only five percent Christian; however, the quality of Catholic life and institutions is said to be quite high. The common explanation is that the refugee Catholics included many of the Catholic hierarchy who had worked throughout the mainland. Since Vatican II, there have been three four-year periods of renewal in Taiwan which have enjoyed the progressive leadership of the hierarchy. Catholic life, according to these priests, appears to be very much on the rise with an excellent dialogue ongoing between the laity and the hierarchy.

The priests tell me that the church in Taiwan is working toward a more indigenous spirituality. There is an extensive dialogue taking place between both the laity and the hierarchy and between Buddhist, Confucian, and to some extent, Taoist believers and Catholics. However most of the latter interreligious dialogue is more the stuff of academic journals. There is little practical use of the spiritual practices of the Chinese religions by native Catholics.

June 26, Taipei

Today I have bussed and walked the city and seen many of the sights. It is hot and humid; there is precious little air-conditioning. I just passed an hour in an air-conditioned coffee shop reading Hunter S. Thompson's piece on Jimmy Carter in the June issue of *Rolling Stone*,[1] which I picked up at the local American military base. Now I am thinking better of Carter, worse of Taipei, and more practically considering how to resolve the case of the "runs" which has come upon me.

Tomorrow I am off to Lion's Head Mountain, said to be a Mount Athos-like concentration of Buddhist monasteries just south of Taipei.

June 27, Lion's Head Mountain

I am sitting on a bench three-quarters of the way up Lion's Head Mountain. I have just walked past six or seven temples and some supposed monastic houses. What I have seen are a slew of tourists, teenagers trekking about with their tape recorders blaring pop tunes, and old nuns selling soda pop by the altars. Only old monks and nuns live on Lion's Head Mountain. The place is quite visibly dying. Cheap shacks selling tourist wares dot the paths to the small compounds that no longer serve as monasteries but as rest stops for the weekender on a vacation. From what I have seen, monastic Buddhism on Taiwan is in a sad, decadent state. I was going to stay tonight at one of the temples but it seemed so much like a highway rest stop that I've decided to travel on.

Tomorrow I am taking a nine-and-a-half-hour bus ride through the mountains of central Taiwan on the East–West Highway. It is said to be a majestic trip through remote back country. I'll stop halfway and spend the night in Lishan.

Δ

1.   Hunter S. Thompson, "Jimmy Carter and the Great Leap of Faith," *Rolling Stone*, No. 214 (1975), 54.

June 28, Lishan

I'm studying the Chinese words for different foods in my guidebook up here in my hotel room before I descend to try my luck in the dining hall. A while ago my hotel room's toilet overflowed. The water level marks on the bathroom wall indicate that this has happened before. Welcome to the Golden Pear Hotel.

Lishan is the only flat piece of land I've seen so far. The ride has been Rocky Mountain spectacular with huge, deep precipices alongside a single-lane road and the usual wild driver. Clouds are making formations *below* the window of my hotel room.

In the evening I met a fellow who told me what he knew about Chinese herbal medicine. He is a student in Taipei and a karate devotee. He told me that the herbal doctor works on a hot–cold principle. Foods that are hot are those that have a high caloric count; cold foods have a low caloric count. For example, meat, fish and sweets are hot, fruits are cold, and most vegetables are middling. These generalizations are far from clear-cut, for tomatoes, pumpkins, and coconuts are all hot. So I think in addition to caloric count, acidity is a factor. Cold foods are used to treat hot illnesses, and vice versa. A hot disease is one that either (1) produces anger (2) produces fever, or (3) stems from taking a hot food. For example, if you have acne which has some basis in oiliness (hot), you should take watermelon or some similar juicy, low caloric-content cold food. If you are angry, cool off with a banana!

June 29, Taipei

The bus trip from Lishan to Tarocco Gorge on the east coast of the island took more than six hours. The combined effect of an old bus with no rear shock absorbers traveling along an incredibly bumpy road etched single lane into the upper reaches of the mountains, a boisterous, not so attentive driver and an absence of guard rails had literally one-quarter of the people aboard vomiting out of the windows before we reached Tarocco Gorge. I spent the first hour of the trip preoccupied with how I would react when the bus rolled off the cliff. After ten minutes of careful planning I had my moves all figured out, how I would lunge my feet to the ceiling and grab the handrail. But then the bus descended for a moment below the cloud level and I got some idea of just how high up we were. It became more practical to pray.

When we got to Tarocco Gorge we headed down through the gorge which is formed by a river running between two vertical rises. It was like being inside a waterfall. A magnificent ride!

At the town of Tarocco my first real adventure in Taiwan began. I had planned to take a bus up the east coast to Suao and then a train the rest of the way to Taipei at the northern tip of the island. However the road to Suao had been recently damaged by an earthquake and no bus could get through. So instead, I decided to hitch the several hundred miles to Suao, walking around the damaged areas on the road. The hitch took me six hours, two of which were spent walking along deserted stretches of the coastal highway. The road was magnificent, again etched high into the mountains with a direct vertical fall to the ocean. Something like the road that travels alongside the ocean at Big Sur in California. The scenery was like the remote mountain country of Hawaii. Every so often the road would dip into a small fishing village inhabited by the aborigines of Taiwan, brightly costumed and tattooed.

At one point I got a ride atop a large truck carrying huge rocks from a quarry. The truck was in procession with fifteen other trucks and the drivers were entertaining themselves by passing one another at the bends along this barely two-laned highway. I passed the time sitting on top of the cab of the truck, like riding an elephant, and looking out over the ocean.

At Suao I got a train to Taipei and made it back to the International House by midnight. Tomorrow I fly to Hong Kong.

... *11*
Hong Kong

July 1, 1976, Hong Kong

Hong Kong rolls out of bed like a well-to-do businessman with the morning off. I've been out on the streets trying to find a coffee shop since seven, but as of seven-thirty nothing seems to be open. So now I'm going to sit in the lobby of the YMCA and wait for the city to rise.

I arrived yesterday afternoon, took a bus to the Y, dropped my bags, and started walking around the city. Hong Kong is a British Crown Colony, and a major staging area for international trade. While strolling about I was continually drawn to window displays and attractive hotel lounges that made me feel like I was in Manhattan. This is a large, wealthy city with more westerners in it than I have seen since leaving the United States two years ago.

This city is a large and sudden step into Western anonymity. In Japan, Korea, and Taiwan, there was a certain kinship among westerners which made me want to smile or wave when I saw another. Here this is no longer possible because there are so many. I was not fully alerted to this fact until this morning, when I received a rebuff in response to my offer of my English language newspaper to a passing westerner.

In Japan it was my custom and that of many others, to hang onto my English language newspaper or magazine after I completed it, and then pass it on to the next westerner I might see. I was always grateful when someone passed one on to me because it gave me something to read while on a train trip or in a cafe. Otherwise there was only Japanese writing all around me and it took a special effort to search out the central areas where papers or magazines in English were sold. Getting something in English while traveling out in the countryside was a special surprise, for there you might not get any

English news for weeks at a time. In Korea, for example, I met a foreigner at Haien-Sa who had been traveling for two weeks. After a lively conversation we both searched our bags and exchanged English language magazines, a *Time* for a *Newsweek*, giving each of us something new to read. In Hong Kong, however, I have discovered that papers and magazines in English are readily available everywhere in the city and that no one appreciates this gesture. I'm sad to have this little ritual come to an end. The kinship is gone.

July 4, Hong Kong

Today on the bicentennial Fourth of July, I ferried with 1,000 members of the Hong Kong American community to a picnic spot out on neighboring Lantau Island. It was great fun. Hot dogs, hamburgers, and ice cream galore topped off by a mock invasion of "redcoats." Midway through the festivities an old sailing ship arrived at our harbor carrying thirty British citizens in colonial dress, attempting to claim the picnic site for England. We settled for a battle out on the football field in which the British incorporated several rugby rules into the game. Nevertheless, the Americans won again.

July 6, Po Lin Temple, Lantau Island

Today I have ferried to Lantau and looked up a fifty-year-old French monk living in a temple near the major Buddhist monastery on the island. The foreign monks at Song Kwang Sa in South Korea told me he was here.

This French monk's story begins with a lung ailment he contracted when he was a high school student living in eastern France. Mountain air was prescribed as an antidote for his illness, so he was sent to live in a mountain village that just happened to be near the Grand Chartreuse, the charter house of Western monasticism's most austere order—the Carthusians. While living in that mountain village, this fellow received his first feel for monastic life by spending some of his spare time in the gallery of the Carthusians' church listening to their offices. He now talks fondly of the Carthusians and of Western monasticism in general. However, at the age of forty, he was stationed in Asia as a journalist for a major French press service. This was when he decided to answer his growing desire for spiritual fulfillment. When I asked him why he chose Buddhism, "Karma" was his only reply.

Starting in Sri Lanka in 1965, this Frenchman studied yoga for four months then went to Nepal to study Tibetan Buddhism for a year. He then traveled to Thailand where he spent five years and was ordained as a Buddhist monk and given the name Dhammarato Bhikku (Bhikku means monk).

In Thailand this temple was in Bangkok, close to the place where Thomas Merton stayed. On the morning before Merton's accidental death by electrocution while attending a conference there, Dhammarato was given a handful of rice by Merton, as he went begging from door to door, and was asked by Merton to return later in the day. When Dhammarato returned, Merton was dead.

After Thailand, Dhammarato came to this little temple in a mountain setting on Lantau. The first year he was here there were two other foreign monks, but they soon left and just a few nuns, the abbot, and he remained. For nine months of the second year, Dhammarato and the abbot sat constantly every day, getting only three or four hours of sleep. The sitting was painful at first, but after awhile Dhammarato says he got used to it. In the seventh month he said that all of a sudden he "came to," and had what seemed to be an enlightenment experience. This was later confirmed when the abbot bowed to Dhammarato's feet and said that the two of them were now equals. This climax in Dhammarato's spiritual journey took place just six months ago. Now he is waiting here for providence to take hold and lead him on to the next stage of his journey. He thinks that he may wind up in the United States, but he doesn't know.

The monastic vows that this monk took in Thailand were not necessarily permanent. He explained that in Thailand monastic vows are in effect only as long as you want to be a monk. You can terminate your commitment (disrobe) at any point and there is apparently little stigma attached. This is in contrast with the Chinese monastic vows that some of the young Chinese now living at this temple have recently taken. As part of their initiation into monastic life they are given a series of cigarette-like scars on the tops of their heads. These are a sign of commitment and a cause for deep shame if they ever break their vows.

Dhammarato Bhikku is an endearing fellow who speaks with real knowledge, insight, and compassion about monastic life in both the East and the West. He says that he would gladly have become a Carthusian, but circumstances led him to Buddhism and the East.

Paying particular attention to purification of the mind, Dhammarato says that it is the same process throughout the world. He talks of the need for obedience so that the mind can remain clear, yet he argues against permanent vows which commit oneself to a vision seen at one stage of the mind's development which may drastically change at another.

During our evening together, Dhammarato spoke to me repeatedly about the necessary evolution of the mind, saying that there are things that we cannot conceive of happening to us now that will occur as we progress. He said that the absolutely worst error we can make is to allow the mind, our consciousness, to stagnate at one level and then assume that our mind's growth is finite.

Dhammarato believes that Buddhism is decaying and dying all over the East. There are pockets of health here and there like Song Kwang Sa in Korea, Po Lin here in Hong Kong, and some places in Thailand and Japan, but things are not going well. He feels that the Communists will soon take Thailand and that other places are threatened by an economic change which is causing a much more secularized society in the more prosperous areas.

July 7, Po Lin Temple, Lantau Island

I rose this morning at four and listened while the monks chanted until five. Then I joined the community for breakfast (nuns on one side, abbot at the head, monks on the other side). Around seven, Dhammarato and I went to sit in the main shrine room. We sat on separate raised platforms, each like a square coffee table with cushions and a roof bearing optional mosquito netting—little portable "Buddha boxes." A nice way to sit.

This is another spectacular temple site. We are on the side of a mountain that drops swiftly to the ocean. A tropical breeze brings a cloudy mist floating incessantly down the mountain. With a setting like this, it is easy to sit.

Today I travel on to the Trappist monastery at the other end of this island.

July 7, Trappist Monastery, Lantau Island

I remember once reading the saga of the Chinese Trappists who were forced off the mainland at the time of the Communist takeover in 1949. Many of them were persecuted and only a minority escaped to Hong Kong, where they started this monastery in exile on Lantau. Once here they found that the land they owned was highly susceptible to erosion. The island rises steeply from the sea and there are few trees. The monks have now mastered that problem through massive plantings of erosion-resistant plants. A further problem is the lack of vocations. This problem is compounded by the fact that almost all of the monks speak

Mandarin, the North China dialect, while almost all prospective monks speak the dialect of South China, Cantonese. Right now there is only one novice. The other fifteen monks are almost all over fifty. The dairy farm that they now have is run by ten lay people. The guesthouse pretty much runs itself with retreat masters coming from outside the community. The advanced age of the monks combined with the great deal of outside assistance they receive contribute to the declining "old folks home" atmosphere of this monastery. They now have financial support from the farm and a sense of stability, but it seems that after years of battling adversity, this little place, nestled in a small valley by the ocean, is just marking time, awaiting its end.

July 8, Aberdeen, Hong Kong

Today I spoke with a twenty-three-year-old seminarian at the only diocesan seminary in Hong Kong. He does zazen and says that there is a recent, broad interest in sitting among the religious, particularly sisters, of Hong Kong. This interest has been catalyzed by two retreats given here by Father Oshida (whom several have referred to in saintly terms) and other retreats given by a fellow named Wong who is slowly introducing all comers to sitting.

Tomorrow morning I continue my frantic pace by leaving for Thailand and a whole new ballgame, headfirst into an area with Chinese and Indian influences.

... *12*

Thailand

July 11, 1976, Bangkok

Bangkok, a sprawling, pulsing, thriving city of four million souls hugging the banks of the Menam Chao Phya thirty miles from the gulf of Siam. "The City of Angels." Glittering, gilded spires of wats (temples) dominate the skyline, like church tops in Rome. The many canals earn it the title "Venice of the East."

Walk through town. All the industrial buildings on corporation row have "spirit houses," elegant little temples devoted to the gods of each piece of land. There are houses on stilts, humped, horned cows on the street, and trucks—big old workaday trucks painted in rainbow colors, and three-wheeled pick-up truck-buses with little barefoot boys as conductors. Small children sell flower garlands on the corners.

On a bus. A little boy with a big paper bag scrounges a seat between two men then turns to each, folds his hands and solemnly bows his thanks. The girl standing next to me wears a Buddha on her necklace as I wear the Virgin Mary. Orange-robed, shaven-headed Hinayana Buddhist monks, barefoot, smoking cigarettes, await tomorrow, the first day of the five-month long Buddhist rainy season (this is a time when the many monks return to their temples for formal instruction and prayer). Monks are forbidden to sit next to women.

Sunset. On a bridge over the main river, I am packed into the tail of a pick-up-truck/bus. People hanging on like bees to a hive. The truck moves with fits and starts through the traffic then suddenly begins to pick up speed. Securing my grip I lean out the back and look over the river and out to the city. Welcome to Bangkok!

Δ

July 11, Bangkok

Since leaving Hong Kong I have flown for three-and-a-half hours around Communist Indochina. I have left the predominate Chinese influence of East Asia and arrived in an area of both Indian and Chinese influences. The major religion here is Hinayana Buddhism. The people are of Chinese–Malaysian stock. Walking about today I relate what I see to what I have heard of India and not so much to what I have already seen in East Asia.

This is Buddhist country. There is little Christianity for, as in Japan, the Buddhism here is formidable competition. There are animistic forms of worship underlying the dominant faith, as seems to be true in all free Asian countries, but Hinayana Buddhism is the predominant religion.

The king of Thailand, while no longer the head of the government, is the defender of the faith, as Queen Elizabeth is the guardian of the Anglican Church in England. I caught sight of the king today in a ceremony marking the beginning of the rainy season. When he entered the wat next to his royal palace, everyone in the huge throng dropped to their knees. He was accompanied by a color guard, shielded from the sun by a blue parasol, and decked out in formal wear. Still he took the time to accept gifts and chat with the people as he walked along the red carpet path leading to the temple's inner sanctum. He seemed like a warm, friendly man and the people appeared to genuinely revere him.

Until 1932 Thailand was an absolute monarchy. Up until recent times all Thai men had to spend a period of time as Buddhist monks. The streets of Bangkok are filled with monks in orange robes. These facts and the profound reverence commanded by the many wats of Bangkok help me to assume that Thailand was once a near theocratic state. What has happened since then, the numerous coups and social unrest, underline the difficulty the country has had in adjusting to anything other than an authoritarian regime.

July 11, Wat Po, Bangkok

This is an ancient temple in the middle of Bangkok. There is a high exterior wall surrounding the city block which the temple occupies. Inside the wall, the wat is like a small city. There are four smaller temples around the main sanctuary. Tacked onto this basic design are many little shrines, burial mounds, and statues as well as little restaurants, schoolrooms, the ancient herbal medical school, and a huge stone phallus worshipped by young women about to marry. The strong impression is that the temple was a city or subcity unto itself not so long ago.

Today being the first day of the rainy season, I have come to witness the evening ceremony. When I entered the temple grounds I was confronted with the sight of several thousand people, each carrying a candle, a stick of incense and a flower, circling the main sanctuary. The monks of the temple were scattered throughout with a small knot of them chanting incessantly over the loudspeaker. People not walking in the procession stood on the side and clasped their hands in prayer. A scene reminiscent of the evening rite at Lourdes (France), where thousands carry candles and walk around the main square while chanting the response to a hymn to the Virgin Mary which is sung over a loudspeaker. Soon the head monk appeared on the dais of the inner sanctuary and addressed the throng. This was a marvelous moment with the temple filled with candles and incense and lay people frozen in attention to the words of the monk. After the address many lingered in the otherworldly atmosphere of the moon and candlelit temple grounds.

July 12, Bangkok

I have just come from a chat with a middle-aged English Buddhist monk whom I ran across at one of the central wats here in Bangkok.

First we spoke about foreign monks in Thailand. This fellow, whose long Thai name I have forgotten, told me that there are now about two hundred foreign monks in Thailand. The first one came in 1958. The Americans are the largest contingent. Some of the Western monks are recently off of drugs, bumming around, hiding from the authorities (with visa problems), or out of money. It used to be easy for a foreigner to become a monk here, but after quite a few bad experiences many of the abbots are sick of young westerners.

We next spoke about the organization of Hinayana Buddhism in Thailand and how in some cases it compared to the organization of the Catholic Church. In the holy city of Bangkok there is a "pope," seven "cardinals," and a group of "bishops." There are also perhaps more ecclesiastical ranks than in Rome. Promotion is made according to scholarly work and seniority. There are not any priests, all are monks, but in the great city temples the emphasis is on scholarly work and little attention is paid to meditation. The city temples are more like centers of academic study than houses of spiritual development.

It is desirable to be a monk, especially if you are poor and have no connections for gaining upward mobility in Thai society. To become a monk you have to: (1) serve a monk for four months; (2) spend two years as a novice; (3) take vows which are in effect only so long as you wish to remain a monk. You may disrobe and then reenter as often as you like. It appears that few of these monks really have spiritual vocations. Instead, they are monks for the time being because it is the accepted thing to do and quite prestigious. If you are a real scholar, you will probably move up in the hierarchy. Still, as a result of this emphasis on scholarship, it often seems that the lay people are the most devout.

My English acquaintance told me that in contrast to the emphasis placed upon scholarship in the city wats, the rural forest hermitages are renowned as centers for spiritual development. There are far fewer monks in these remote temples, yet this is apparently where the truly spiritual monks and the outstanding meditation teachers can be found. Several of the more serious westerners are concentrated in one such hermitage in Ubon, not far from the Mekong River and Cambodia. There they are studying with a Western meditation teacher. The Englishman suggested that I take a trip out there to see what is going on.

July 13, Ubon

A week before I left Japan, I received a letter from Father Thomas stating that the Spencer monastery was recently visited by an American Thai Buddhist monk. This fellow, Phra Sumedha Bhikku, said he had been living as a monk in Thailand for the past thirteen years. In the letter, Father Thomas included the monk's address so I could look him up when he returned to Thailand. From Japan I wrote him and while I was staying at my hotel in Bangkok, I received an invitation to visit his temple in Ubon. This monk now turns out to be the same one referred to by my English friend as a foreign teacher of Thai meditation. Today I have traveled west to visit his community.

To get here I took an all night train eastward across this tropical country to the city of Ubon, just fifty miles away from Communist-infiltrated hamlets by the Mekong River. I then hailed a three-wheeled taxi and rode out to this little forest temple directed by Phra Sumedha Bhikku and populated, I have learned, exclusively by foreigners, including two Catholic priests.

Phra Sumedha Bhikku is in his mid-thirties. He was raised as an Anglican in San Diego, California. He says that as a child he liked Christianity but felt stifled and fearful of his high Anglican priest. He became interested in the East and took up South Asian studies in the early sixties while a student at the University of California. Shortly thereafter he received an M.A. in his field and left for Peace Corps service in Borneo. After two years in the Peace Corps he traveled to Thailand and in the mid-sixties decided to stay there and become a Buddhist monk. As a pioneer among foreign monks, Ajahn (honorific meaning teacher) Sumedha, studied among forest monks in remote temples in northern Thailand. His present teacher, Ajahn Chah, runs the main temple, about an hour from here, with which this side temple is affiliated. About a year ago Ajahn Chah entrusted Ajahn Sumedha with the leadership of this place and declared it exclusively for foreigners. When word of this was passed around, about twenty foreign monks, then scattered throughout the hills of remote Thailand, came here to study.

Two of the monks are former American soldiers who were stationed in Vietnam. One has been here for five years or five rainy seasons (as monks here mark the time). This fellow told me that he will soon complete the required time of formation and then will be permitted to be a wandering monk. He is apprehensive about leaving the security of his home temple and wandering, but he said that he is even more apprehensive about returning home to the United States. His parents have been here and still keep in touch, and he hopes that soon he will feel sufficiently secure in his Thai monastic discipline to be able to return home and not lose all that he has learned.

Of the two priests, both of whom are French, one appears to be pursuing Thai Buddhism in a manner similar to Father Luke's pursuit of Zen Buddhism back in Japan. This fellow has been on the Buddhist monastic trail for five years. The other priest is a missionary for an outfit called the Paris Foreign Missions. He is spending three months here so that he might better understand Buddhism. Both have shaved their heads but still say Mass every week or so, though they say there are technical difficulties.

One of the novices is a black American from Florida.

Another Western monk is a Frenchman who was raised as a Catholic. Like Ajahn Sumedha, he too says that as a child he was attracted to the atmosphere of Christianity but was driven away from it by the hell and brimstone preachings of his priest. He now believes that the Catholic faith is profound, but that when he was young none of the people who were teaching him the faith knew that depth. He told me that French children are given superficial instruction in the catechism all the way through adolescence and on to young adulthood. They then marry, have children, and the cycle repeats. There is not a deeper teaching for adults. The French monk bitterly laments never being exposed to the deeper aspects of Christianity by his priest. "Must not the priest be a guru?" he asked.

July 13, Ubon

After spending a day with these twenty young men, they still look peculiar, with their bare feet, orange robes, shaven heads and eyebrows, and towering above the much shorter Thai villagers. In the evening Ajahn Sumedha reads to them from holy books both East and West. Recently they have been reading Carlos Castenada's fourth book *Tales of Power.*[1] Seeing them all huddled together at night in their little bamboo shrine room, Ajahn Sumedha reading aloud, I think of Peter Pan and his merry band off in Never-Never Land.

On the other hand, these men have displayed a great deal of courage to persevere under a rigorous regime of moral discipline and spiritual effort. Unlike the foreigners who do zazen in Japan with relatively few organizational buttresses, these foreign Thai monks must resolutely follow the rules for forest monks plus the rules of their home temple. The Hinayana Buddhists emphasize two aspects in their Buddhism: (1) *Dhamma* (wisdom), and (2) *Vinaya* (moral discipline). The Vinaya is actually the name of the book that outlines the various rules that govern all aspects of a monk's life. It provides the structure to which is added Dhamma, through meditation and spiritual guidance. Because of all the monastic rules, Thai monks are dependent upon nearby villagers for their survival. Monks are forbidden to do such things as dig in the garden, make their own meals, or build their own shelters. So the lay people do almost all of the manual work and in return are said to build up "merit," much like Catholics garner indulgences.

When I asked Ajahn Sumedha about the need for all of these rules, he told me that they were necessary to help the monk form new habits. The rules are particular because they attempt to meet every old behavior with a new one and thus hopefully help the new monk to lead a more spiritual life. Ajahn Sumedha told me that he was aware of the problem of following the rules solely for their own sake and not realizing the spiritual frame of mind they are supposed to engender. He says he is continually talking to the monks about keeping a balanced attitude toward the rules. Still the dominant effort is to break with the past and the rules seem essential to this end.

Somewhat similar to the rules that the Thai monk must follow are the many guidelines of St. Benedict's Rule followed by Western monks. In contrast to the Benedictine Rule and the Vinaya are the few rules that Zen students must follow and, at the most extreme, the complete absence of rules

---

1.   Carlos Castenada, *Tales of Power* (New York: Simon and Schuster, 1974).

at Father Oshida's community. On the one hand, the two monastic sets of rules emphasize an outer scaffolding that the monks eventually internalize, on the other hand the Zen students and Father Oshida place emphasis on intensive contemplation in the belief that essential aspects of these monastic rules will be both discovered and internalized in the course of each person's spiritual evolution. This is fundamentally a question of the Spirit and the Law, which to emphasize, for whom, and in what circumstance. Answers vary.

In this hot, humid forest hermitage, all of the rules seem to have taken the crust off of these men and made them perhaps more vulnerable and reflective than they were when they arrived. There is a disciplined moderation to their lifestyle. They seem easy-going yet austere, hospitable yet focused upon their spiritual life, the closest thing I've seen to a Trappist way of life in Buddhism.

The monks follow this schedule:

3:00 A.M.	Rise
3:10–4:00	Chant
4:00–5:00	Meditate
5:00–10:00	Begging and meal
10:00–3:00	Meditate in huts
3:00–4:00	Chores
4:00–5:00	Walking meditation
5:00–7:00	Meditate in huts
7:00–8:00	Hot drink and meditate together
8:00–8:30	Chanting, talk or reading
8:30–9:30	Sit together

Each monk has a small hut, raised from the ground on stilts and made of bamboo. These huts are scattered throughout the forest around the large, open-air shelter which serves as the dining hall and meeting room. In addition to these buildings, there is a small shrine room where they do their chanting and have the evening meeting. During the time for meditation in their huts, the monks follow through on whatever spiritual advice Ajahn Sumedha has given them. In the afternoon everyone comes together for walking meditation. This is done by each monk by picking out two trees or two spots about fifteen yards apart and quietly walking back and forth between them.

The great challenge of the forest monk's life is complying with all of the many rules and rigorously following through on meditation practice. I imagine that it would be difficult to live here without relying heavily on meditation. You almost have to see life from a more spiritual point of view to endure in this environment.

A portion of the day is spent begging for food. Today I followed along as the monks split into groups and begged along their preassigned routes. The group I chose to follow walked single file into the local village to collect food for their only meal of the day. The village consisted largely of bamboo houses raised on stilts and cut into a clearing in the jungle. We followed a mud-packed path from house to house where people with food offerings, mostly rice, knelt to receive us. The villagers do not stand, for then they would be taller than the monks (though some of the taller westerners would still dwarf them), instead they look away from the monks' eyes and bow when the monks pass. The begging route I followed wove through two or three villages and took about an hour to complete. When we returned the food was taken to a shelter where some townspeople had come to prepare it. Since I was not an ordained monk, I was allowed to handle the food bowls and offer food to the monks, actions that their rules forbid them to do. The whole meal was an elaborate ritual in which I had to be sure never to have my head above those of the monks. Afterwards there was some chanting and then all disbursed to their huts.

During a conversation with the French monk this afternoon, I said that there was no doctrine of grace in Buddhism. He denied this by saying there was a notion of grace, the "grace of the guru" in Tibetan Buddhism. The "grace of the guru" he said is similar to Catholics praying to saints. He said that in Tibetan Buddhism there is a supreme guru of each sect or lineage who is appealed to by monks to assist them in their practice. If one does not progress, then it can be said that he or she has not been graced by the guru. Similarly, the guru can shine down upon some person who may not appear to be worthy to receive the guru's blessings. Grace in Tibetan Buddhism, according to the French monk, is a belief in the abilities of gurus now dead to bring their powers to either assist or trouble the devotee.

Late this afternoon, I had another talk with Ajahn Sumedha. He told me that the primary difference between the Buddhism practiced in Ceylon and Thailand (Hinayana) from the Buddhism practiced in China, Korea, Japan, and other places in Southeast Asia (Mahayana) was the emphasis that Hinayana places upon moral discipline. Ajahn Sumedha told me that Americans are very much interested in the spirit and disciplines that encourage the raising of consciousness, but they are not in favor of moral discipline. He thinks that it is absurd for people to think that they can be simultaneously loose in their morals and disciplined in their practice of meditation. The one tears down while the other builds up, and so you do not get anywhere. He says that one of the problems in Mahayana Buddhism and also with the spiritual interests of young Americans is that they do not have an even balance between their moral discipline and their meditation practice. Zen might give you the wisdom, but it does not tell you how to handle it. Hinayana, according to Ajahn Sumedha, gives you both.

July 15, Ubon

After a few days with the foreign monks out here in Ubon, the mosquitoes and the food are driving me away. I need a bath, some air-conditioning, and a long snooze. It takes quite a bit of motivation for anyone to survive in this jungle. For a westerner to stay for thirteen years is really remarkable. Ajahn Sumedha *is* a remarkable fellow. He is well respected among his Thai peers and yet he transcends the culture to speak the Hinayana wisdom to his foreign monks and visitors alike. Like Dhammarato Bhikku, the French monk in Hong Kong, I look forward to seeing him when and if he comes to the United States. With the Communists threatening Thailand, it may not be long before all of the foreign monks have to leave.

July 16, Bangkok

I flushed myself clean with ten trips to the bathroom on the night train back from Ubon. Now at seven in the morning I have checked into a decent hotel in Bangkok and am about to go to sleep. I am sick. What the monks gather in their begging bowls is what I ate in my one meal each day. Not by any Western standards is it clean, plus it came from a high-risk typhoid area during the rainy season, an awful risk. All of the monks at Ubon were said to have had at least one serious disease or another (malaria was common), but that was just one more thing they endured to be there. I think I'll rest here in the hotel for a day or two before pushing on for a tourist's visit to Chiang Mai in northern Thailand.

July 18, Chiang Mai

After a sleepless night on an air-conditioned bus with seats nowhere near my size, I got to Chiang Mai this morning intent upon getting a good day's sleep. Soon, however, I discovered that my wonderful little $1.50 a night hotel rented small motorcycles for five dollars a day. So right away off I went to explore Chiang Mai. In the late morning I drove up the mountain behind this city and continued beyond it to the villages of the Meo tribe. The hills around Chiang Mai are filled with many different tribes that hundreds of years ago settled in the rippled valleys and hillsides of this rugged northern Thailand terrain. The tribes remain distinct, and the great adventure for visitors is to backpack out into the countryside for a few days to visit the villages. After riding all around the city and surrounding areas on my motorcycle today, this evening I have hooked up with a couple of Australians and we're going to join with several others and a guide for a three-day backpacking trip through the hills up near the Burma border.

July 21, Near the Burma Border

It is six in the morning. I'm sitting on a chair outside the thatched hut where several of us slept last night here in the Lisu village. There are roosters nearby, giving notice to the dawn. I just went down to brush my teeth in the little waterfall area of the nearby stream but ran across a French couple doing a shower in the altogether, so now I'm back up here with the roosters.

This is the beginning of day two of the hill tribe tour. Yesterday a whole busload of young and hardy German, French, and Australian tourists, and me, the only American, headed out from Chiang Mai. We drove about a hundred miles, had our passports checked when we got near the border, switched to a dugout boat ride for an hour or so, walked two miles inland and now we are rising from sleep at the Lisu village.

Today the plan is to trek all over the place for seven hours. We are going to see a number of different villages, take pictures, and distribute candy. I'm not much for going. I feel too much like the white "candy man" viewing the "primitives," as though they were in cages in a museum.

We are heading back to Chiang Mai tomorrow and then I will grab a night bus to Bangkok. The next morning I have a reservation on a flight to Hong Kong, then a few days later my charter will leave for New York. So this is my last letter from Asia.

Epilogue

Nearly a year has passed since I left Asia. In late July I made my connecting flight from Bangkok to Hong Kong and boarded a charter flight that flew to Anchorage and on to New York. In New York I took a shuttle flight to Hartford and then hitched to the Trappist abbey in Spencer, Massachusetts.

Aboard the flight from Hong Kong, I resolved to enter the Spencer monastery. The idea had been growing since visiting the French monk Dhammarato Bhikku that last June. He helped me set aside my ambivalence and see my future in black and white. If I was really serious about deepening my faith, I should cease my restless wanderings and throw in my lot with a like-minded band in an austere monastic setting. I mentioned this to Father Thomas in a letter that June and now I looked forward to discussing my desire with him personally.

While not committing himself one way or the other, Father Thomas allowed me to begin the procedure leading to monastic entrance. This began that week with a series of interviews with the members of the monastery's vocational board. The information gathered from these sessions was augmented by similar interviews five months later and by a battery of psychological tests administered soon after.

By February 1977, seven months after returning from Asia, I appeared to have passed through the qualifying rounds and was now considered a prospect for the Trappist life. The next step was to begin a month-long observership in March and after that, if all was still going well, plunge into the six months of postulancy, then two years of novitiate, and on to the more permanent stages of commitment.

With my thoughts riveted on monastic sanctuary, I passed an uncomfortable autumn and winter at my parent's home in Ann Arbor, Michigan. My resolution to enter the monastery was an intensely personal decision which I was unable to explain effectively to my parents. Instead, I tried to avoid the subject and deal with it only if I had to. That time never really came, for at the end of the first week of my monastic stay, I chose not to become a monk.

My reasons for seeking a monastic way of life had, by that March, proven to be more psychological than religious. In my earlier contact with the Trappists, before setting out for Asia, the abbey had symbolized an oasis of order and tranquility. The peace of the cloister and the counsel of Father Thomas provided a needed rudder for my postcollege life. Now, however, several years later, my personal life had been set aright through Zen meditation and the sacraments and I found that my seemingly deep-seated need for monastic retreat had lessened. Yet this was not an obvious transition. How I came to question my monastic vocation is recounted through the journal notes I kept during those seven days.

Tuesday, March 1, 1977, Spencer

Hulking along with my eighty-pound suitcase stuffed with books, Bibles, and clothing, I bummed a ride from where the Worcester bus had left me in downtown Spencer for the two-mile hike north to the abbey. The driver of the old red Chevy who picked me up said he was from Chicago but had settled in Spencer some fifteen years ago. As we drove along he offered that the first time he had been to the abbey church was the previous year when his brother visited from Chicago and wanted to drop by. The only other time he had been up that way, he said, was to go hunting on the more remote parts of the monastery's twelve hundred plus acres.

I got out at the Trappist gift shop by the highway sign announcing "St. Joseph's Abbey—Trappists" and went in to ask the presiding monk if he could drive my suitcase up the hill when he got off work in a half-hour. Brother James was on duty. He sticks out in my memory for the time he told me that weather was weather and that people should enjoy its diversity rather than complain (that was just after I had complained). James said that he would take the suitcase up, but then we saw Brother Albert driving his truck up the hill and signaled to him to stop to give me a lift. I jumped in with him and he took me to the cottage within the cloister where the candidates stay.

Dropping my bag in the cottage and finding no one about, I headed up to the guesthouse kitchen where Father William was setting up for dinner. Father William, a scholar who entered the monastery after some time as a parish priest, spends a good part of every day serving the needs of the lay retreatants. He had recently made a series of tapes on contemplative prayer that often serve as the foundation of the retreats he gives to the weekend or week-long visitors. Father William good-naturedly said that it was about time I arrived (they had me scheduled to be there on Sunday). This must have been an error in my letter to Father Xavier, the vocational director. As I was turning to leave William, Father Mark walked by. Mark, in his fifties, is the community's physician, having entered the monastery soon after completing his internship. He attended me when I was laid up for several weeks with a bad back in the summer of 1974. He is also a Zen fan and friend of Lucien Miller, an Asia academic at the University of Massachusetts. Through Lucien, Mark has helped to set up several meetings between Eastern masters and monks of the abbey. Mark was interested in my letters from Japan. He told me that a woman who had recently visited Spencer said she had spent some time with Father Oshida's community. Mark and I only talked for a minute before we had to go to the church for Vespers.

When I got to the church I nudged Xavier to let him know I was there. In a mock-stern manner Xavier replied, "It's about time." I then found a place in the choir. Because I was now a candidate for entry and have successfully passed through the preliminary two rounds of interviews with the vocational board, I was allowed to stand in the choir with the monks. My apparel, however, was not as elegant as the flowing, white robes of those who stood alongside me. Instead I had to be satisfied with my work shoes, jeans, and down winter jacket. As I sat and rose through the Vespers choreography, my odd presence in that row of white robes was underlined by the leak of tiny white feathers through a hole in the arm of my jacket. This caused down to filter out each time I raised my arms and a white "fairy dust" to descend upon the heads of my angelic companions.

Singing along with the hymns, I found that I could not concentrate on their content. This has been a disturbing phenomenon with me throughout the past year. I do not recall the content of ritual hymns and readings in church services. This does not mean that I am distracted and thinking of other things (though there is more than enough of that) but rather that I am not intellectually apprehending what is being said. I sing the notes, pronounce the words, and attend to the moment, but none of it registers. At Mass I try to attend to the homily readings, still when someone wants to discuss what was said I invariably draw a blank—yet I *am* paying attention.

After Vespers I went to see Father Thomas, whom I had run across on the way to the office. We went to the upstairs room of his bilevel living quarters built into one corner of the cloister. Father Thomas had just returned from visiting Spencer's Berryville, Virginia daughterhouse and was home for Lent before heading for Europe for the General Chapter meeting of all Cistercian abbots in Rome. After some talk of how I spent my winter at home, I raised the question of my recently completed psychological tests. On Monday I received the results from the psychologist who had administered them in Boston, and frankly, I told Father Thomas, they left me feeling flawed. I went on to ask Father Thomas to look closely at the results of the tests and to draw out anything that he felt was serious and would give me trouble in adjusting to the Trappist life. He said that he had yet to see the results of these tests, so we could not discuss them for a few days.

Father Thomas had to get down to supper before the kitchen closed, so I left and walked back to the cottage. There I ran across Xavier. We talked further about the results of my tests and he reassured me that everyone came out feeling flawed after hearing the results, and that I shouldn't worry about it. Feeling better, I headed into my room to lie down before Compline, the final office of the day.

When I closed the door to my room behind me, my head was pounding with a headache and I was already pondering leaving the monastery, yet I knew that this reaction was only characteristic of my several monastic stays. The initial hours and days of adjustment to the Trappist life have always produced an immense rebellion in me. True to form, I lay down in bed and began to map out a whole new direction for my life and buttress it with persuasive rationale. This had happened so many times before, however, that I knew I should not take these first impulses seriously. Rather wait a few days when, as before, more balanced thinking would come to the fore.

Nevertheless I began to worry about the results of the psychological tests. They had revealed that my normal social behavior is to be withdrawn. This did not seem normal for me; rather it was something that I now attributed to my intense seeking. A second trait was a pronounced pacifism, an easy-goingness and unwillingness to initiate that leads to my withdrawal from contested issues rather than taking a stand. This was another characteristic trait of late that I had heretofore explained away as an unwillingness to argue unimportant ideas (the only important issues being vital religious ones that concerned me). These negative traits may prove to be contemplative ones, I thought. Still I felt flawed.

On the positive side of the ledger, the tests showed that I had a contemplative temperament. And I had a tough, solid self-confidence that would do me well in taking the psychological toll of monastic adjustment.

With these results in the foreground, I went on to wonder what it was that really called me to this life. When I first came to the abbey, and subsequently spent time in Father Thomas' counsel, it was partly an attempt to counterbalance the turbulence of my college years. Now, five years later, I led a fairly stable life, did zazen twice a day, and went to daily Mass. There was an integration and strength in my life that was absent several years ago. Before I sought monastic serenity to counterbalance college insanity. Now my life was better balanced, so where was the monastic call?

I fidgeted in bed for several hours with these thoughts then began to fantasize what I would do if I didn't follow through on this monastic course. Random thoughts led me to going to graduate school and getting married in Boulder, Colorado. Though I've never been there, I've heard good things about that town.

Wednesday

This morning I woke up at three for Vigils, my head still throbbing and thinking of Boulder, and made my way to the office. Afterward, my jacket still puffing down, I headed for the chapter room where Zen fans do their sitting. I arrived early, lit the candle and stick of incense at one end of the room, and soon was joined in setting up my cushions by Father Edward John. Edward John was my friend in zazen that summer of 1974. It was good to see him, we smiled, then in the candlelit shadows got down to sitting. We sat facing each other, ten feet apart. He rang a bell and away we went, mixing together longer periods of zazen with shorter periods of kinhin. Around five we were joined by Father Basil Pennington, *the* scholar of the house, and young Damian, a novice. We sat again until five-thirty, chanted *"Kyrie Eleison"* and prostrated ourselves three times. Then Edward John, Basil and I left, and Damian continued.

Back in the cottage, the sun was just beginning to appear on the horizon. The silence of the morning and the blueness of the sky enshrouded my solitary presence looking out over the fields from my room's window. But my thoughts were far from silent. I had already pretty much decided not to be a monk, the only question now being how long I should remain on retreat. And yet I knew that, as before, this disposition would change.

Lauds, Mass, and breakfast came and went. I worked dusting in the church and the chapter room, then at 2:30, after the office of None, I caught sight of Father Thomas and asked to see him after Vespers. Xavier had scheduled me to see Father Joseph, the novice master, on Thursday and the vocational board was to meet Friday to review my candidacy, so I thought I had better air my doubts with Father Thomas right away.

Father Thomas and I began our talk by my mentioning my difficulty in digesting the intellectual content of the office Psalms, hymns, and readings. He said that while not the norm, my condition was all right as long as I was attentive and not off on other thoughts. I told Father Thomas that it was not that I did not want to read them, it was just that I could not. Moreover, even the most enticing article or book had became arduous for me after only a page or two. This was also true of conversation which was of a superficial or abstract nature. Instead conversation needed to be vital to my experience to keep me attentive. Father Thomas seemed concerned and suggested too much reading in college for the current possible balancing out. Perhaps, but it had been going on for more than a year now. We would have to pursue this further.

Next I brought up the lack of psychological motivation for my monastic vocation. Father Thomas pointed out that ultimately the call does not come from me at all but from God and at first I may not hear it at all. This is another point we will have to pursue in greater depth. It seems essential that one have a nonexperiential theological foundation for leading this life, a base built on Christ, but what leads one specifically to a monastery is still beyond me. After witnessing the departure of five solemnly professed (permanently vowed) monks since I have been in touch with the abbey and on balance listening to the myriad reasons for why a man becomes a monk and how he perseveres, I acknowledge that there is a monastic path but it seems to be ever so subtle, mysterious, and beyond my reason to perceive.

Leaving Father Thomas I walked up to the guesthouse and ran across Father Basil Byrne, the evening's guestmaster, on the way. Basil told me that he had just spent the afternoon talking to a Jewish Transcendental Meditation instructor about a book called *A Course in Miracles*.[1] He said he had been talking theology with this fellow and his friends for the past two hours and now was just trying to ease himself out of those thoughts. In his careful, grandfatherly manner, Basil sadly told me that the TM fellow had forsaken his Jewish heritage, hooked into TM, and now was pondering the occult. Rather than go through all that they had discussed, Basil summed up his feelings by saying that you've got to have roots. The

---

1.   Marianne Williamson, *A Course in Miracles* (Glen Ellen, Calif.: Foundation for Inner Peace, 1976).

fellow with whom he had been speaking was far off of the ground, far from his roots, his religious heritage, and getting into the occult was only taking him farther up and afloat.

Thursday

After breakfast this morning I went over to Father Joseph's office. He has been the novice master for a good part of his nearly twenty years at the abbey. Joseph is Vietnamese. He comes from a large Catholic family in a village near Hanoi and was the rector of a seminary there before being sent by his superiors to study economics in New York City. While there, he felt drawn to the monastery and soon entered.

Father Joseph and I went over the ground I covered yesterday with Father Thomas and then we pushed on to more general topics. I told him that I was so tired of the Zen–Christian subject that if there were a renowned Zen master in downtown Spencer I did not think I would want to see him. Zen no longer fascinated me. I did not want to see any more gurus or masters. I would rather just sit. In discussing making a life commitment to the Trappist way, Joseph had no hard line to force on me. He encouraged me to take one step at a time. Though committed himself to remain a monk, Joseph said that he thought other, more temporary, lifestyles possible for those with nonmonastic vocations.

Friday

The vocational board met for some time this morning to consider my candidacy. Afterward I met with Father Xavier to discuss the results. Xavier began by noting the conclusions drawn by the psychologist who administered my tests, who had said that I was a good candidate for the Trappist life, though I was still riding out my postconversion fervor and would need a great deal of community support when I finally settled into the Trappist life. In this vein the board noted that since my conversion I had not put down roots. I had not held a career job or become involved in a local parish and so had probably not yet fully integrated my conversion experience with normal life. The implication was that my vocation might be premature. In the light of these reflections, the vocational board came up with two recommendations. First, it suggested that Father Raphael, a monk and a trained psychiatrist, and I go over the test results in detail. Second, they advised that with Father Raphael's consent, I take an extended observership of three-months duration during which I could further assess my commitment to their life.

After banking on monastic sanctuary for so many months, I was surprised that my response to the board's findings was more elation than chagrin. I walked out of Father Xavier's office filled with relief. I cannot dispute any of the board's insights. In fact, their reading seems so appropriate that offering the three-month observership rather than ouster may be just an act of charity intended to slowly awaken me to the possibility that my life was not supposed to be played out as a monk. If I am not, a least for the present time, to be a monk, then the Board's news is an important catalyst toward helping me discover just where God wants me. But I am moving too fast; I have yet to see Father Raphael.

Friday evening

I have been at the abbey only four full days yet, as predicted, I have already ridden a psychological roller coaster. My thoughts are of two strikingly different modes. When I am thinking of becoming a monk, my mood becomes somber, diligent, but rich in the fullness of contemplation. I have a vivid perception of the great majesty of the spiritual life. While among the monks I have a greater sense of heartfelt love and communal support. Everything takes on an ethereal light. I feel vulnerable yet detached from my ego and merged with the monastery's transcendent peace.

On the other hand, when my candidacy appears not to be faring so well, my thoughts turn to how I should lead my life on the outside. For some reason I think of Boulder, a university community like my hometown of Ann Arbor, yet nearer the mountains and great open spaces and not far from Spencer's daughterhouse in Snowmass, Colorado. I think of going to the university there to get some graduate degree that would assist me in helping people. I imagine plugging myself into the local Newman Center and keeping up with my zazen. How I will move into a vegetarian co-op, keep up my jogging, and be more outgoing with others. How I will date and be sociable. And I wonder about marriage. It goes on and on.

With no monastic rigor buttressing my actions, I also sense putting off more for the future. I am more ego-centered, I plan for the survival of my self and less for the growth of my soul. I feel less humble and vulnerable and more self-assertive and strong. The sense of awe and majesty of the spiritual life diminishes to a blind impulse to be sure to get in my sitting and make it to daily Mass.

Saturday

This morning I came to my meeting with Father Raphael with a great deal of respect for this monk-psychiatrist's powers of perception. Father Raphael had been vital to my movement toward conversion in 1974 and, in my visit to Spencer this last December, a brief meeting with him had again made me feel that he could help me to fashion a more sensible, broader view of my life. I trusted him.

After going over the salient results of the psychological tests, Raphael affirmed my genuine attraction to the monastery but offered that this interest had been enlarged beyond its real dimensions by the withdrawal and lack of initiative I had demonstrated in my interactions with others. This withdrawal had probably overintensified my desire to withdraw to the monastery. My agreement with Raphael's suggestion was less intellectual and more emotional. Indeed the climax of our meeting came when I asked him if all this meant that I did not *have* to become a monk. His simple answer "Yes," gave vent to oceans of relief.

Several hours later I found myself wondering just what is the monastic calling. With my own calling now appearing less genuine than before, I wondered, what is it that calls a young man to the monastery? Human reason buckles under the weight of such a question. God calls a man to the monastery. But why one more than another and only a few rather than everyone?

Perhaps all of us are called, but only a few perceive it. We may or may not stumble upon this realization as we amble through life. And what if we do? Does that mean we go to the monastery? How many are there out there who are called and are answering but are not in monasteries? What are they doing?

Monday

This afternoon I had a second long session with Father Raphael. We discussed the role of Zen meditation in my Christian prayer life. I told Raphael that zazen *was* my prayer life. I did go to daily Mass and read the Gospels but practiced no other forms of prayer. Raphael asked what I did to reach God in the time between meditations. To this I admitted that I had rarely spoken to God in prayer. Rather I have trusted my meditation efforts to bring me closer to him than words might allow. Raphael persisted, "You are not always at such an intimate level of devotion, are you?" This was emphatically true and indeed there were many days when I found contact with the Lord impossible even through an hour of silent meditation.

Raphael appeared to be saying that I needed to see my moments of silence in relation to the other, more verbal forms of prayer that help me to reach that silence. The time between meditations needs to be buttressed with discursive (conceptual) prayer so that I keep from falling too far away from the will of God. Zen meditation for Christians, he said, must be solidly founded on Gospel reading, the sacraments, discursive, and petitionary (asking for God's guidance and grace) prayer, rather than standing alone without foundation. Though I may have real and sublime experiences of God's love, without solid roots in the teachings of my faith I run the real risk of becoming disembodied, so detached from my religion, culture, and social setting that I am neither more fully human nor more fully divine, rather I float about like a helium balloon in some psychic no man's land.

Through a series of questions Raphael established that I was on the verge of such an experience. Drawing from the fact that I did little discursive prayer, had not read a book in over a year, and was finding it quite difficult to digest the content of homilies and readings, Raphael offered that the source of my growing anti-intellectualism was my singular focus upon zazen. Since this problem with Christians doing zazen was one that I had noted previously in others, I thought that I was alert to its occurrence. But this seems not to be the case.

Still I argued vehemently with Raphael. Why should I engage in discursive prayer if I can readily leap this initial stage and enter into the intimacy of zazen? Talking to God and doing such things as the rosary now seem so silly if I can have a far deeper experience through meditation. In a stunning reply, Raphael noted that discursive prayer *must* be part of the contemplative process. If I was not aware of doing it now, I was probably repressing it. My verbal petitions to God were being repressed, it appeared, by an arrogant reliance solely upon zazen.

Though I left his office in a rebellious mood, it rapidly dawned on me that Father Raphael's counsel pierced to the heart of the matter. I was being arrogant in steadfastly refusing to use verbal prayer. And so, during the remainder of the day, I tried several times to "talk to God." This felt silly and it seemed at first like I was out of my depth; yet gradually verbal prayer became less alien. I continued to do it because of the arrogance I now perceived in my singular zazen approach, but it was not long before "talking to God" yielded its own motivation. I found that calling on the Lord in the midst of the day's activities kept me more easily focused on his love. I could more easily draw on his strength.

Δ

Tuesday

My ambivalence toward discursive prayer was still with me when I went to conclude my sessions with Father Raphael this morning. However, this apprehension was overridden by the feeling that Raphael and I had little more to discuss. It was time for me to leave. I reported my experiences with "talking to God" the previous day, Raphael encouraged me to stick with it, and I agreed. But more importantly we both sensed that my monastic stay had come to a close and that I was on the threshold of a new beginning. Yes, I will go out more to others, and yes, I will practice discursive prayer, but now it is obvious that I will not practice these things here.

I will be leaving the monastery today. I have not been asked to, nor have I really made the decision, rather this seems to be the natural next step. For the time being, my business with Spencer is completed. I need to go home and digest this experience. More importantly I need to begin a needed reconciliation with my family, my community, and my local church which has been for so long postponed.

And what of those larger issues of Zen and Christianity? There is certainly a movement afoot in the United States to bring about a greater Christian openness to the East. Several of the monks of this monastery have been working to integrate their knowledge of Eastern techniques with the Western spiritual traditions. Their efforts have found fruit in a book by Father Basil Pennington, *Daily We Touch Him*,[2] a series of cassette tapes on "Contemplative Prayer" by Father William Menninger, and a number of workshops on practical religious experience led by these men, by Father Thomas, and by other monks of the abbey. There is also talk of a separate lay monastic community that might be mothered by St. Joseph's and serve as a meeting ground for East and West—a place that would allow practical instructions, counsel, and dialogue to occur among Christians who are exploring Eastern approaches to their faith. And

---

2. Basil Pennington, O.C.S.O., *Daily We Touch Him* (Garden City, New York: Doubleday and Co. Inc, 1977).

finally, there will soon be a meeting in Petersham, Massachusetts of several American and European abbots, monks, priests, and interested lay people, in an attempt to make real headway in the East–West monastic dialogue at home here in America.

Surely there are good things to come. But no dialogue can come about if the participants are not first firmly rooted in their own community, culture, and spiritual tradition. This has been the lesson of these past seven days, and too, perhaps, the greater lesson of my Asian journey.

Afterword

Twenty years have passed since I left the Spencer monastery in that spring of 1977. I did not go to Boulder but to Berkeley, California where I re-entered "the world" through the Master of Divinity program at the Jesuit School of Theology.[1] There I joined a small band of lay people in training for ministry in the Catholic Church. As my studies progressed, however, I became interested in the sociology of religion and American religious history. After Berkeley, I went on to pursue a doctorate at Emory University in Atlanta. I am now married and a professor in the religion department at the University of Florida in Gainesville.

Throughout these years I have continued in my practice of meditation and Christianity. In Berkeley I met Dan O'Hanlon, S.J., and joined in his early morning sessions of meditation and Mass. I have continued to do retreats at St. Benedict's Monastery, Spencer's daughterhouse in Snowmass, Colorado, and with the Vipassana Buddhist's Insight Meditation Society in Barre, Massachusetts. The new frontier for me is the integration of spirituality into daily life. In Gainesville, regular practice and a group of like-minded friends continue to nurture me in this effort.

Much has changed at Spencer as well. Following the period of experimentation with Eastern practices has come a renewed attention to the Christian mystical tradition. Under the direction of two new abbots, Father Paschal (1981–1983) and Father Augustine (1983–1996), the riches of the monks of the Christian East, the Desert Fathers, the Cistercian Fathers, and Western Catholic contemplative spirituality have become more exclusively central to the teachings of the monastery. In 1981 Father Thomas resigned as abbot and went to live at Snowmass, where he has become the leading voice in the Centering Prayer movement and the founder of Contemplative Outreach.

---

1.   David G. Hackett, "Lay Catholics at the Seminary," *America*, September 16, 1978, 158-160

Centering Prayer has its origins in the early 1970s. As Father Thomas recalls, this was a time when Eastern masters were attracting a great number of young people with well-thought-out and well-presented methods of meditation. Although thousands were going to India every summer in search of spirituality and a guru, very few of them thought of inquiring at a Catholic monastery. Part of the problem was the state of Catholic spirituality which at that time "locked up" the contemplative tradition within the highly restricted monastic cloister. Yet even then this vibrant spiritual tradition often existed in only a truncated form with an emphasis on monastic observances rather than on the interior transformation to which these practices are meant to lead. The rest of the problem had to do with the absence of a Catholic "how to" method of contemplative practice that could provide people with the kind of spiritual experience that was available through the methods of Eastern masters.[2]

In 1973 Father William Menninger, at that time the monastery's guest-master, began working out just such a method for meditation based on the richness of the fourteenth century spiritual classic *The Cloud of Unknowing*. Initially this method was intended for priests and nuns but gradually, as it was refined by Fathers William, Thomas, and Basil, it attracted Catholic and Protestant laity hungering for the experience of contemplation. The response was so positive that an increasing number of workshops were offered and an advanced workshop was developed by Father Thomas to train teachers of the method.[3]

In 1981, when Father Thomas moved to St. Benedict's Monastery, he continued to respond to requests to share Centering Prayer in various parts of the country as well as a new desire for a more intensive Centering Prayer experience. Because of this burgeoning interest, in 1984 Father Thomas established Contemplative Outreach to coordinate efforts to introduce the Centering Prayer method to people seeking a deeper life of

---

2. Thomas Keating, *Intimacy with God* (New York: Crossroad, 1994), 112-28

3. The name "Centering Prayer," was coined by Father Basil Pennington who recalled the frequent counsel in Thomas Merton's writings to "return to our own center and pass through that center into the very center of God." On the origins of Centering Prayer, see "The Origins and Inspirations of Centering Prayer" by Fathers Basil Pennington, Thomas Keating, and William Menninger. This audio tape is available from A.M.M. 5580 Havana St., Unit #6A, Denver, Colo. 80239. Among the growing number of books concerning Centering Prayer, see especially Thomas Keating, *Open Mind, Open Heart* (New York: Amity House, 1986) and *Invitation to Love* (Rockport, Mass.: Element, 1994); also Basil Pennington, *Centering Prayer* (Doubleday, 1980) and *Call to the Center* (Hyde Park, N.Y.: New York City, 1994).

prayer and to provide a support system capable of sustaining their commitment. In 1986 a national office of Contemplative Outreach was established and at present there are thirty-seven active national and international regions. At the same time, Thomas has responded to those seeking a deeper experience by developing a series of ten-day intensive, postintensive, and advanced-intensive retreats. For ten years he was also spiritual guide to the residents of Chrysalis House, a live-in community in Warwick, New York, that until quite recently offered formation in Centering Prayer and contemplative living.[4]

And what of the Christian–Buddhist dialogue? From what I have been able to gather, the conversation in Japan continues though some of the principals, Fathers Lassalle and Dumoulin among them, have passed away. Father Oshida is still farming and praying with his community in Takamori. In Europe, the Zen retreat houses started by Father Lassalle continue to flourish. Here in the United States, Father Thomas has been a moving force behind the Monastic Interreligious Dialogue.[5] This organization, formed from the North American Board for East–West Relations at the Petersham conference in 1978, encourages participation of North American monastics in the encounter between Eastern religions and Christianity by developing conversations and sponsoring mutual exchanges between monks of different religions. During the summer of 1996 representatives of Buddhism's three main schools met with their Christian contemplative counterparts at Gethsemani, the Cistercian monastery in Kentucky where Thomas Merston lived, to discuss the "Christian/Buddhist Dialogue on Meditation." According to Father Kevin Hunt of Spencer, one participant in this meeting: "Right now there is developing a very rich exchange between Christians and Buddhists." At the same time a whole new generation of scholarship continues to enrich and advance the Christian–Buddhist conversation.[6]

---

4.   Contemplative Outreach can be reached at the following address and phone number: 9 William Street, P.O. Box 737, Butler, N.J. 07405. Tel: (201) 838–3384.

5.   MID's newsletter, *The Bulletin*, is published three times a year and is available by subscription from the Monastic Interreligious Dialogue, Our Lady of Grace Monastery, 1402 Southern Avenue, Beech Grove, Ind. 46107-1197.

6.   Some of the most recent books include: Robert E. Kennedy, *Zen Spirit, Christian Spirit* (New York: Continuum, 1995); Robert Aitken and David Steindl-Rast, *The Ground We Share: Everyday Practice, Christian and Buddhist* (Boston: Shambhala, 1996); and Thich Nhat Hanh, *Living Buddha, Living Christ* (New York: Riverhead, 1995).